ADAPTABLE STAGE COSTUME
FOR WOMEN

ADAPTABLE STAGE COSTUME FOR WOMEN

A hundred-in-one costumes

designed by

Elizabeth Russell

NEW YORK
THEATRE ARTS BOOKS

First published in 1974
by THEATRE ARTS BOOKS
333 Sixth Avenue
New York 10014

© 1974 ELIZABETH RUSSELL

ISBN 0-87830-007-4

Library of Congress Catalog Card No. 73-75920

Printed in Great Britain by
The Bowering Press Ltd.
Plymouth

CONTENTS

ILLUSTRATIONS
OF COMPLETE COSTUMES

LAYOUTS

Note: All these on squared paper in inches.

MAKING-UP DIAGRAMS

MATERIALS

English	American
Fablon (trade name)	Contact paper (for wall)
Felt-backed Fablon	Contact felt (for wall)
Repp: a furnishing fabric used for curtains or 'drapes'	Repp
Dupion (trade name), also a furnishing fabric for curtains or 'drapes'	Antique Satin (Siam, Bali, Penang etc.)
Felt: used mostly for handicrafts: not as important as the furnishing fabrics	Felt
Nylon millinery net (McCulloch and Wallis, Dering Street, Oxford Street, London W1A 1EX)	

METRIC CONVERSION TABLE (approximate)

Inches	Centimetres	Inches	Centimetres	Inches	Centimetres
$\frac{1}{2}$	1·3	$6\frac{1}{2}$	16·5	20	51
$\frac{3}{4}$	2·0	7	18	21	53·5
1	2·5	$7\frac{1}{2}$	19	22	56
$1\frac{1}{4}$	3	8	20	23	58·5
$1\frac{1}{2}$	4	$8\frac{1}{2}$	21·5	24	61
2	5	9	23	26	66
$2\frac{1}{2}$	6·5	10	25·5	27	68·5
3	7·5	12	30·5	28	71
4	10	13	33	30	76
$4\frac{1}{2}$	11	14	35·5	36	91·5
5	12·5	15	38	38	96·5
$5\frac{1}{2}$	13·5	16	40·5	42	106·5
6	15	18	45·5	45	114

Inches	Centimetres	Ounces	Grams
48	122	1	28
92	234		

Yards	Centimetres	Pints	Millilitres
$\frac{1}{8}$	11·5	1	568
$\frac{3}{4}$	68·5		
$1\frac{1}{4}$	114		
$1\frac{1}{2}$	137		

CHAPTER I

PROS AND CONS AND ECONOMIES

MAKING costumes for the stage can be a most exciting and rewarding job, it is an adventure into a world of colour and effects that are not possible in the clothes of the rushed and practical world of today. Not that practicality has no part in stage costume: on the contrary it plays a very large and vital part.

Good costume design must reproduce the effect of a period without the discomforts; wood, whalebone, horsehair padding must be replaced by modern stiffenings and paddings, but still achieve the line and effects of the earlier unwieldy materials. The costumes must be so well fitted that complete ease and comfort are felt by the wearers, and so secure that no gesture however dramatic will derange them.

Three vital points must therefore be borne in mind. Good fit, good colour, and good line, for then the costume will look right whether seen close to, or more important, as the audience will see it, at a distance. A distilled essence of a period must be the objective, rather than the reproduction of masses of finicky details.

Many Dramatic Societies and Groups do not find it financially practical to make their own costumes. They reckon that to make a dress will cost as much as to hire it, and as its use may be limited to one production, are therefore prepared to put up with the problems of clothes that do not fit properly, with the resultant bad appearance, often because the right size was not available in the colour needed for the part. Also there is the great disadvantage to the cast who, because the budget only allows for one week's hire, never have the chance to become used to the costume of the period they are portraying, and are therefore unable to make actions match their words and the needs of the costume, in the close dramatic harmony of a really good performance.

If costumes are made, the Wardrobe Mistress, having worked hard to produce lovely dresses, then finds that in the interests of economy they must all be unpicked and made over to meet the needs of another period production; and while making costumes is most interesting and rewarding work, unpicking, which often means spoiling careful work in the process, is as frustrating as it is damaging to the materials, and after one or two changes of style the dress may well become a write-off. As a woman's figure has a variety of curves, and a greater variation in the size of these curves, getting a hired costume to fit properly is naturally more difficult than for a man's figure, where apart from change of size, the only other major point of change will be the waistline. But though men's shapes do not vary so drastically the fashion of their clothes did; it varied so sharply that no continuous basic line emerges. Consider the difference in shape between the doublet and trunk-hose of Elizabethan times, with the breeches, embroidered waistcoat and cut-away coat of the mid-eighteenth century.

But it is not the difficulty of making all these different styles that is the biggest problem, there are various adjuncts to male attire that are almost impossible to make, and certainly not if economy has to be considered. For instance, swords were not only used for killing people, they were an essential part of every "gentleman's" apparel, and changed with the fashion as much as clothes. If they are made of wood they don't sound right if there is a fight, and even where there is no fighting they rarely look right. Boots and shoes are another big problem, and their shape changed as much as any other item of dress, and with men they are very much on view. There are the slashed, blunt-toed shoes of Henry VIII's reign, the great topped boots of the Cavaliers, and the high-heeled shoes of the eighteenth century, to mention but a few. They can often be hired separately but one cannot blame the costumier if the charge is relatively high, as the costume is usually hired as a whole, and it will be found that the separate items cost nearly as much as the entire outfit would have done.

Long experience has led to the conclusion that it is better to hire costumes for the men, and make those needed for the women, especially as this can be done with no sacrifice of standards of appearance or accuracy, in fact quite the contrary. In designing the Adaptable Costume cost, the ease with which the basic dress can be changed in size and fit, have all been worked out to the last detail and put through stringent tests on the stage, and also by wearing a costume while giving the Talk and Demonstration about this method of making costumes. The basic dress forms a permanent framework to which can be added the sleeves, collars, ruffs, bodice additions and a variety of underskirts, correct for the period of the play which is being produced. Moreover they do not have to be made in a rush, a 'basic' wardrobe can be built up as and when time and money permit, the 'additions' are then the only things that have to be made before a production.

One final point, there is an old saying in the theatre, that an actress cannot play Juliet well until she is old enough to play the Nurse. There is certainly an element of truth in this saying. How often the slightly older actress loses a part she could play very well, because modern clothes do nothing to help conceal what time may have done to a chin line, or the size of the hips. This is where costume plays are such a help. Head-dresses, caps, and bonnets are all held in place by chin supporting straps, or bows of ribbon. Full skirts conceal the increased hip size, and ruffs and fill-ins soften the line at the throat.

Where there are all women in a drama group, they can even play men's parts in a costume play. Nell Gwynne did, and was much admired in them by Mr. Pepys; she probably had very nice legs!

What might be called the 'fitted bodice and full skirt' periods range from 1461 (Edward IV) to the latter part of Victoria's reign in 1885, with the exception of the extreme change in dress, inspired by Greek costume that became fashionable during and after the French Revolution. This fashion came to England in a milder, though not much warmer version during the Regency period at the beginning of the nineteenth century. The fashion, though charming did not have a long life, the climate of Northern Europe soon made it necessary to add spencers, pelisses and shawls, and the diaphanous Greek-inspired gown faded from the scene. Even before Victoria came to the throne the fitted bodice and full skirt was back in favour, and remained so till 1885, after which another big change of line began, skirts became slimmer and, though at first dresses were over-trimmed, clothes were gradually affected by the more active life women began to lead.

But the bodice-and-full-skirt was the basic shape in all those other periods, which from the drama point of view are so important: the Tudors who, whether good or bad, have made such wonderful subjects for plays, Shakespeare, the Restoration Comedies, and the plays of Goldsmith and Sheridan in the eighteenth century, till we come to the Victorian period about which so many plays are now being written.

It might be thought that always using a basic dress, and tied therefore to its range of colours, must make for lack of variety, but this in fact is not the case. The 'basic' dress is always the background on which are 'painted', as it were, all the changes which added colours, variety of fabrics and trimmings can make. Add velvet, fur, lace and jewels and you have a dress for a Queen, keep it very plain with the most simply styled additions needed to mark the change of period, and a country woman is the result.

Another advantage is, that because of its inter-changeability fewer whole dresses are needed, a consideration where storage space is a problem. The 'additions', sleeves, underskirts, etc, can be kept in boxes, each labelled according to their period, which are much easier to store than rows of costumes.

There are two other basic shapes, one is the fitted gown which was worn from Saxon times till 1410 (Henry IV) when several different styles were fashionable, though the gown was still worn at court, elaborately trimmed with fur and jewels, till about 1460. Saxon women wore a simply shaped tunic over the gown, so that only the sleeves and lower part of the dress showed. The Norman women at first wore the same fitted gown, in fact the only difference in their dress was the long semi-circular or straight cloak, fastened with a cord or ornament. If Saxon women wore a cloak it was on the lines of the pancho cloaks of today, but circular with a hole for the head and falling to knee level.

During the early Norman period (William I and II) a simple head-dress of veiling was worn, held in place by a band or cord. It was head-dresses that marked the greatest change in fashion over the next centuries, becoming more and more complex till they evolved into the fantastic styles of Henry IV's reign. The sleeves were either long and tight, or wide, sloping from the dropped arm-hole join, to end at the wrist, and were at times very wide indeed. But when the Surcoat became fashionable in 1307, sleeves were always tight fitting and extended over the hands. The Surcoat was at first like a sleeveless over-dress cut away at the sides from shoulder to hip level, and worn over the fitted gown. As time went by it became very elaborate till it gave way first, to the Houppelande, and then to the high waisted, full skirted dress of 1461.

The other basic shape is the Greek chiton; Helen of Troy is said to have excelled at weaving them, it is virtually a wide tube of material either tunic length or reaching from shoulder to ankle, held in place at the shoulder in various ways, and crossed with strappings to hold it to the body. Sheets, joined at the sides, and ornamented with painted designs can be very effective indeed, and with practice can be draped in a variety of ways.

Whichever period is being dressed it is the 'line' that must be kept clearly in mind, for it is this that conveys the impression of accuracy; real accuracy would be too expensive, difficult, and too uncomfortable for the actress to wear. Imagine breathing with a piece of carved wood under the material and trimmings of your stomacher, or shaving the hair back from the forehead in order to wear one of the more extreme head-dresses fashionable in the reigns of Edward V and Richard

III. Selecting the right styles and reproducing them credibly but comfortably is the object of good costume design. Whatever costumes are being made they must be seen on the stage, under full lighting plot well before the dress rehearsal. Lights often play tricks and so does distance, they can in fact completely change the effect, and it must be remembered that stage clothes are always seen at a distance with the result that good line and colour are of paramount importance, and good line inevitably involves good fit. When choosing colours take into account the fact that most blues 'die' on the stage; only the very clear ones with no vestige of red in them or with some green, will survive stage lighting. Yellows tend to soften; rusts and greens hold their colour; purple darkens under some lighting but it always looks rich; clear slightly pinky mauve looks fresh; and both pink and red hold their own, and so does orange. Some reds darken but like purple give a rich effect; crimson red, however, should not be chosen for a basic dress, as at one period it was only permitted to be worn by noble or Royal personages. Suggestions for colours are given at the end of Chapter II for the 'Fitted Gown' and in Chapter III for the 'Basic Bodice and Skirt'.

Nearly all drama groups and societies have to watch their budget and wise spending can save a lot of needless waste. Very often cheap, thin material is bought to 'save' money, only to find that it must be underlined, which means spending more money in the long run. Even after good sense and economy has been practised in buying materials, extravagance can break out in the trimmings. It is not necessary for instance, to buy expensive gold and silver trimmings, old furnishing braid or lace can be painted with gold or silver paint. Look for such items at Jumble Sales. 'Ribbons' need not be ribbon but Prussian or straight binding, which is less than half the price, and can be bought in a good range of colours and two widths. Webbing painted in an appropriate design, and ornamented with a few beads will make a handsome belt or edging. The heaviest weight Vilene is a good stiffener as it does not wilt, while the millinery nylon net is a must for many head-dresses, and polyester foam, carved to shape with a sharp knife, then covered is wonderful for padding, being both light to wear and stiff. Crepe paper is another effective form of trimming, especially for the ruching worn on eighteenth- and nineteenth-century dresses. When sewing it use either stranded cotton, or a very long stitch if a machine is used. Fichus are easily made from plain or frilled edged nylon curtain net; the remnant counter will often yield the $1\frac{1}{2}$ or $1\frac{1}{4}$ yards needed and a wide piece will make the sleeve frills as well. It is useful to have easily washed material close to the neck as make-up rubs off most in this area. For this reason ruffs, though made up on a linen or cotton band are best made of plastic tablecloths cut into strips, choosing a cloth with a lace-like edge for the ruffs of rich people. A paper taffeta petticoat is also excellent for this purpose if you are lucky enough to have one, or find one at a Jumble Sale, both the plastic and the taffeta wash very easily and need no starching or ironing.

Always allow a good hem on skirts so that if the bottom needs to stand out stiffly, as it was required to do in Henry VIII's and Elizabeth's time, a fold of newspaper can be inserted in the hem which will give the desired effect, and the resulting slight rustle when walking will sound like silk petticoats. It is essential to buy the right type of material for the basic dresses otherwise the proper line cannot be achieved.

For the Fitted Gown soft, but *not* thin, fabric should be used. Brushed rayon,

WILLIAM I. 1066~   ILLUSTRATION NO1.

SAXON.   NORMAN.

HENRY I. 1100-54.

wool and rayon mixtures, and woollen jersey if it is not too expensive, are all suitable, but do not use nylon jersey as the warmth of the body under the heat of stage lights may cause it to cling in very unbecoming places. Plain bedspreads, if two single ones can be found, also the cheaper and therefore softer furnishing Repps are good, especially if used on the cross. For the surcoat that was later worn over the fitted gown, a heavier fabric should be used though it must not be stiff, as at first the surcoat followed the soft line of the gown. As a guide to what is 'soft' or 'stiff', pull the material on the cross; if it stretches easily it is 'soft'; if it does not stretch, or very little, it is 'stiff'; the thinness of the material is not the test.

For the Basic Bodice and Skirt much stiffer fabric is required to produce the right line. Furnishing Repp is again a very good choice but the heavier quality should be used, and Dupion is another excellent material to look for in the furnishing department. Owing to the method of weaving the reverse side is a different shade so there is a second choice of colour. Both these fabrics are available in a wide range of colours, and are pretty reliable in their repeats if more of the material is needed. Don't be tempted to economise by buying the cheaper and lighter weight materials, look for the 'discontinued lines' which are very much reduced in price. Go to the remnant counter and look for matching lengths, but they must be not less than $1\frac{1}{4}$ yards or multiples of that amount, the only exception being $\frac{3}{4}$-yard lengths which are enough to make most sleeves. Look on market stalls for odd lengths of velvet, brocade and patterned materials, where they can often be found at very reasonable prices, and as plain colours should be used for the basic or gown it will not be difficult to find materials that will blend or contrast thus giving an entirely new effect with each addition.

The Jumble Sale is another happy hunting ground for so many of the things needed for stage costumes, from old straw and felt hats to cretonne curtains for seventeenth- and eighteenth-century underskirts, odd pieces of velvet and fur which add a regal look to fifteenth- and sixteenth-century costumes. Indeed a wise Wardrobe Mistress will ensure 'first pick' by sending round a pleasant letter asking well-wishers if they would give old sheets, curtains, bedspreads, lace and lace-edged petticoats, also bits of costume jewellery and pearls to the Drama Group or Society. A great deal of money will be saved in this way, and the donors will be amazed and pleased when they see what exciting things have been made with the help of their gifts.

In the U.S.A. some of these materials have different names:

English	American	Notes
Fablon (a trade mark)	Contact paper	(for wall)
Felt-backed Fablon	Contact felt	(for wall)
Repp	Repp	A furnishing fabric used for curtains or 'drapes'
Dupion (a trade name)	Antique satin (Siam, Bali, Penang, etc.)	Also a furnishing fabric for curtains or 'drapes'
Felt	Felt	Used mostly for handicrafts: not as important as the furnishing fabrics

CHAPTER II

THE BASIC FITTED GOWN

THE GOWN fitted the figure closely from shoulder to hip, then flared out full to the ground. As it was not joined at the hip line, and only laced at the back for fit, it is difficult to see quite how this shape was achieved. The most likely explanation is that, as most dresses at that time were made of woollen material, it was easy to shrink the upper part of the dress, leaving the lower part unshrunken, and therefore fuller. Now-a-days materials are either pre-shrunk or unshrinkable so another way must be found, and the most practical alternative is a wide, long dart at the centre back and centre front, as well as side shaping. The placket, fastened by hooks and bar eyes should be in the left-side under-arm seam, and extend to hip level. If a zip is used it must be well masked, and one 12 or 14 inches long will be needed. The centre back dart seam is masked by lacing which, though not used, will serve as ornament, and look very authentic at the same time. The centre front dart seam will also be partly masked by the trimming which encircles the neck and front opening, which extends to bust level (see illustration). Both darts are 2 inches wide on the double thickness of the material at the neck edge, and continue this width till they reach the waist then slope off to nothing 9 or 10 inches below the natural waistline (see Lay-out 1, pp. 8-9). The arm-hole is not shaped and the sleeves, whether wide or tight, are joined to the gown at the dropped shoulder level (see Diagram 1, p. 11).

The front of the gown is cut 2 inches longer than the back and a dart made under the arm from the side seam out to the bust, and can be made bigger if extra shaping is needed (see Diagram 1 for sleeve join). The side seam is sloped out to the hem of the dress as far as the material will permit (see Layout 1) and then an extension piece added to achieve the required fullness. A 2 inch wide turning must be allowed on all side seams as this is the only point at which the gown can be enlarged, the sleeves must have the same width of turning so that they can be let out to the same extent as the side seam, otherwise the sleeve top and the dropped sleeve-line would not be the same size.

The gown was not only trimmed at the neck, but at the end of the sleeves and sometimes where the sleeve was joined to the gown, as well as round the hem. This trimming was usually embroidery, and can be simulated very effectively by a design painted onto webbing in suitable colours. Do not paint the design direct onto the dress, as if the gown is worn for a later period with the surcoat, it then had little or no trimming on it, the surcoat had all the ornamentation. Poster paint or Gouache give good results. When the gown was worn with a wide sleeve the tight sleeve of the under-tunic was visible at the wrist, for this the long sleeve of a jumper or cardigan cut off above the elbow and hemmed, with elastic run through the hem will give the desired effect and save the cost of an

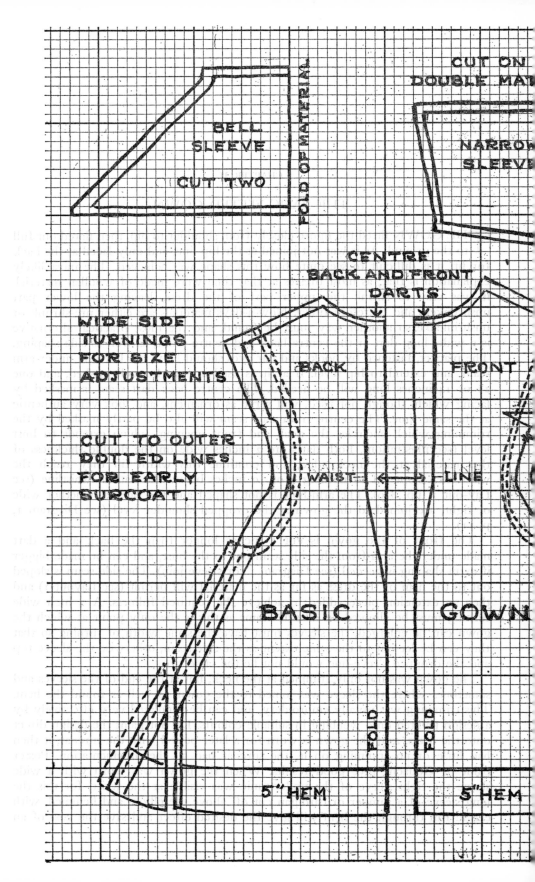

BELL
SLEEVE

CUT TWO

FOLD OF MATERIAL

CUT ON
DOUBLE MAT

NARROW
SLEEVE

CENTRE
BACK AND FRONT
DARTS

WIDE SIDE
TURNINGS
FOR SIZE
ADJUSTMENTS

BACK

FRONT

CUT TO OUTER
DOTTED LINES
FOR EARLY
SURCOAT.

WAIST ⟵⟶ LINE

BASIC   GOWN

FOLD

FOLD

5" HEM

5" HEM

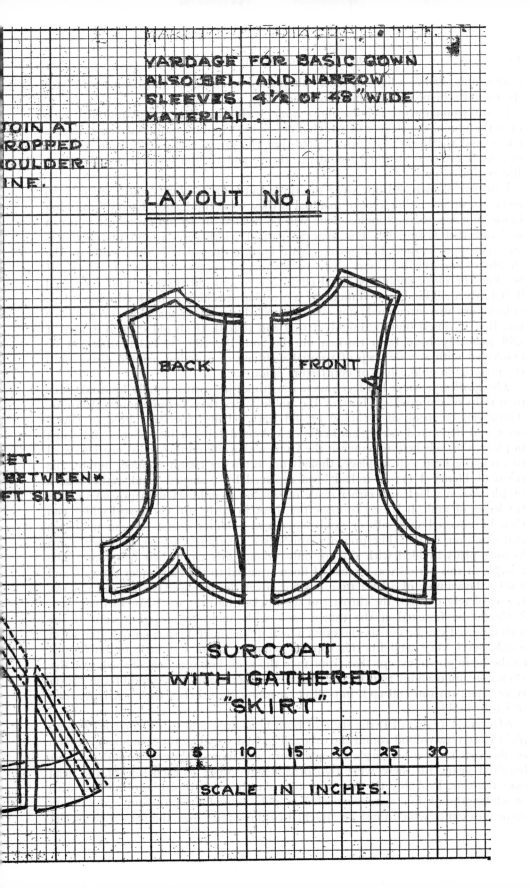

YARDAGE FOR BASIC GOWN
ALSO BELL AND NARROW
SLEEVES 4½ OF 48" WIDE
MATERIAL.

JOIN AT
DROPPED
SHOULDER
LINE.

LAYOUT No 1.

BACK   FRONT

ET.
BETWEEN*
FT SIDE.

SURCOAT
WITH GATHERED
"SKIRT"

0   5   10   15   20   25   30

SCALE IN INCHES.

under-tunic. Either a light or dark colour may be chosen so long as it fits in with the colour scheme of the whole costume.

Saxon women wore a loose short *tunic* with wide sleeves and rounded neck over the gown, the sleeves of which were tight. The bottom of the tunic, sleeves and round the neck were ornamented, but the gown was usually quite plain; a soft head *veil* was swathed round the throat and tucked into the neckline (see Illustration 1, p. 5).

Norman women did not wear the tunic but wore a *cloak*. These are easy to make but do use rather a lot of material as they were full length. Heavy furnishing fabric, not less than 48 inches wide will be needed, or an old curtain if you can find one that is suitable. The material is held width-ways round the shoulders and the upper corners held apart with a cord, a deep dart is then made on the shoulders and the back cut away to the neck-line (see Diagram 1, p. 11). If possible the cloak should be lined edge to edge, an old sheet will do very well if it is dyed. This is not difficult if a washing machine is used, provided dark colours are not attempted, nor will it spoil the washing machine for ordinary use, if it is rinsed out thoroughly (tried and tested). If an old curtain is used it will probably have been thrown out because the edge is faded, this can be concealed with a wide strip of painted webbing or a design painted direct onto the material in gold, silver or contrasting colours.

The *girdles*, worn at hip level, were sometimes just ornamentally knotted cords or a strip of embroidery, but for the noble ladies they became more elaborate. These can be made of webbing or old leather belts especially 'gold or silver' ones, and decorated with glass beads or coloured foil cut into shapes and stuck in place, the ends held together at the front with a silk cord. A cord was also used to keep the head veil in place, though not often by Saxon women, but by the reign of Henry I (1100) it had been replaced by a shaped band, rather like a simple crown which was either made of silk, or of gold set with precious stones for ladies of rank. It is easy to make the shape in fairly stiff cardboard which can then be covered with silk or gold paper, and coloured metal foil cut in shapes and stuck on, to look like precious stones (see Diagram 2, p. 13). Hair was worn in long plaits braided with ribbon; only young girls wore their hair loose. The *wimple* of this period was a piece of linen attached to the hair under the veil, and unlike the wimple of a later time did not cover the forehead (see Layout 2, p. 16). It completely covered the throat and was tucked into the neck-line of the gown; it should be fastened at the centre back with hooks or snap fasteners. If the material used can be cut on the cross it will drape much better; an old, thin sheet would serve very well for this type of wimple. There was little or no change to the basic gown, except that from 1350 the neck-line was boat shaped. For this alteration undo about two inches of the shoulder seams and some of the centre front seam, turn in and tack into place, masking the stitches with a narrow strip of fur or braid.

After 1272 (Edward I) the style of both head-dress and hair changed, the long plaits were now wound round the ears and looked very like the 'ear-phone' fashion of the 1920's. This hair style became more and more elaborate during the next hundred years, till there were two ornamental 'cones' at each side of the head over the ears. Probably the best way to make these is by plaiting false hair with equal lengths of fine wire concealed in gold or coloured ribbon, and shaping them into cones which must be attached to the circlet over the ears. This circlet

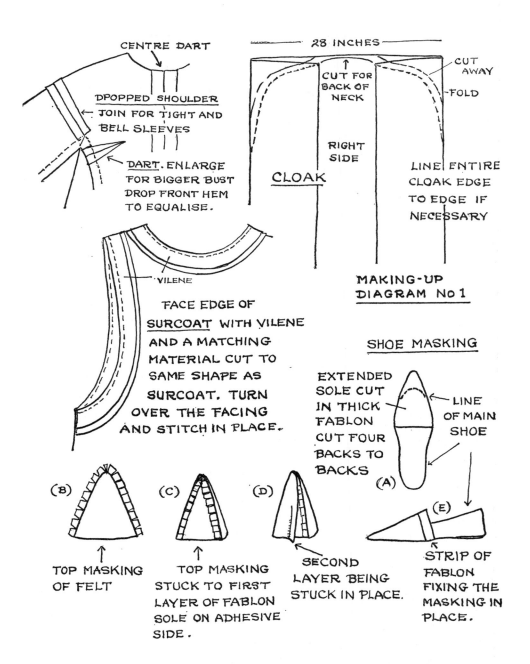

CENTRE DART

DROPPED SHOULDER
← JOIN FOR TIGHT AND
BELL SLEEVES

DART. ENLARGE
FOR BIGGER BUST
DROP FRONT HEM
TO EQUALISE.

- 28 INCHES -

CUT FOR
BACK OF
NECK

CUT
AWAY

FOLD

RIGHT
SIDE

CLOAK

LINE ENTIRE
CLOAK EDGE
TO EDGE IF
NECESSARY

VILENE

FACE EDGE OF
SURCOAT WITH VILENE
AND A MATCHING
MATERIAL CUT TO
SAME SHAPE AS
SURCOAT. TURN
OVER THE FACING
AND STITCH IN PLACE.

MAKING-UP
DIAGRAM No 1

SHOE MASKING

EXTENDED
SOLE CUT
IN THICK
FABLON
CUT FOUR
BACKS TO
BACKS

LINE
OF MAIN
SHOE

(A)

(B)

TOP MASKING
OF FELT

(C)

TOP MASKING
STUCK TO FIRST
LAYER OF FABLON
SOLE ON ADHESIVE
SIDE.

(D)

SECOND
LAYER BEING
STUCK IN PLACE.

(E)

STRIP OF
FABLON
FIXING THE
MASKING IN
PLACE.

was of course only worn by ladies of rank. An extra piece of wire should be run up through each cone to keep the plaits in place, and a strip of braid, sometimes studded with jewels, could be stitched to the outer edge of the cone to enhance the effect. The actresses' own hair must be held in under the cones, and a veil was sometimes worn draped over the back of the head and fixed to the points of the cones.

After 1410 an elaborate *canopy* covered the cones of hair instead of only a veil. To construct this rather difficult head-dress first make a foundation of Vilene or felt as shown in Diagram 3A, p. 17, or an old felt hat can be used if one can be found with a deep enough crown. Next cut three layers of the nylon millinery net to make the half cones that are better, and lighter than cones of hair for this head-dress. The layers of net (see Diagram 3B for shape and measurements) must have hat wire button-holed on all round the edge, then be covered with crêpe hair which is criss-crossed with gold or silver ribbon, lightly stitched into place. The edge of the half-cones of net are then bound with bias binding to match the crêpe hair, this covers the wire and the ends of the criss-crossed ribbons. Lastly add a strip of ornamental braid to the bottom curve (see Diagram 3C) which is then sewn to the corresponding curve of the foundation. Finally make the 'canopy' top by covering an oval of thin cardboard with a patterned material, allowing ¾-inch turning all round. Notch, turn over, and stick onto the underside, which should then be covered with a non-slippery material. Felt-backed Fablon would be a good choice as it is self-adhesive, and would also strengthen the top (see Diagram 3D). Cut 4 inch wide strips on the bias of the same material as the top; if joins are necessary arrange to have them at the back or sides. Fold in half lengthways, turning over a narrow hem on each edge, slip-stitch to the covered top (see Diagram 3E). Then with double thread, stitch the apex of each half-cone to the edge of the canopy top at the sides, and also attach it to the foundation with a few strong stitches at the centre top. This will strengthen the head-dress and also make it dip in the middle as the style required.

With all these head-dresses a flesh-coloured strip of ribbon should be sewn to the bottom of each cone and fastened under the chin; never use elastic—it had not been invented, and cannot here be concealed. It is fortunate that this not very becoming head-dress is rarely worn, even in professional productions. A wise Wardrobe Mistress will learn to keep a delicate balance between historical exactness, and making the best of an actress's appearance. A little tactful licence may sometimes be taken when fashions are hard to wear, except by the young and beautiful. *The Surcoat* (see Illustration 2, p. 15) which became fashionable about 1307, was made on the same lines as the basic gown, but cut away at the sides from shoulder to hip (see Layout 1, pp. 8–9). It should be made of heavy material or lined with old sheeting. The cut away sides must be faced back with a 2 inch wide section of Vilene, the same shape as the surcoat, this will prevent the sides from sagging. The Vilene must also be faced with material that matches the colour of the surcoat (see Diagram 1, p. 11). By 1390 the style of the surcoat had changed, it was no longer cut in one piece from shoulder to hem, but had a skirt-like part gathered onto the top just below hip level. If possible it should be made of heavy Repp or woollen material (an old winter coat could be used for the top part) and was often trimmed with fur. The skirt section can be of lighter weight material for it did not match the top, but complemented it. For ladies at court the top part would have been ornamented with gold and jewels,

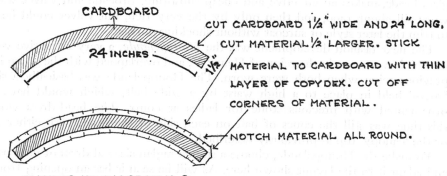

CARDBOARD

24 INCHES

1½"

CUT CARDBOARD 1½" WIDE AND 24" LONG,
CUT MATERIAL ½" LARGER. STICK
MATERIAL TO CARDBOARD WITH THIN
LAYER OF COPYDEX. CUT OFF
CORNERS OF MATERIAL.

NOTCH MATERIAL ALL ROUND.

MAKING-UP DIAGRAM No 2.

MITRE CORNERS AND STICK
MATERIAL DOWN, PRESSING
IN PLACE WITH THE FINGERS
TO MAKE A SMOOTH EDGE.

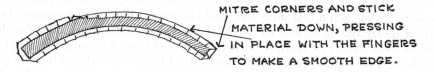

BACK

HOLD IN PLACE WITH BRASS PAPER
FASTENERS, TO FIT HEAD.

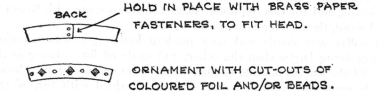

ORNAMENT WITH CUT-OUTS OF
COLOURED FOIL AND/OR BEADS.

THE SAME METHOD IS USED FOR CROWNS AND 1320 HEADRESS.

STIFFEN CARDBOARD WITH HAT-WIRE
HELD IN PLACE BY STICKING DOWN TURNING
OF MATERIAL. BACK WITH
SELF-ADHESIVE FABLON
AFTER THE TIE-ENDS
HAVE BEEN STUCK
IN PLACE. THESE MUST
BE LONG ENOUGH TO
KNOT UNDER THE CHIN,
AND WIDE ENOUGH TO
COVER THE EARS. HOLD
IN PLACE WITH BRASS PAPER
FASTENERS.

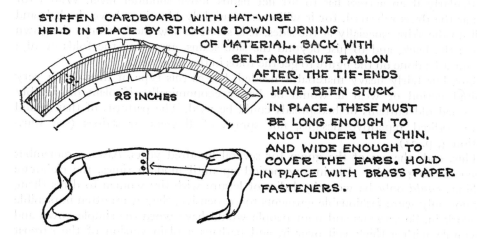

28 INCHES

for which buttons covered with gold or coloured foil, and stitched in place with glass beads, makes an effective and cheap substitute. Brocade and velvet was not worn till about 1400, and then only by the very rich, but velvet could be used to trim the later style of surcoat without shocking purists.

The next fashion development was the *Houppelande*, a very attractive version of which was worn in the reign of Henry V, and overlapped with the gown in the previous reign when both were worn. The Houppelande was basically a simple 'gown' held in place to a high waist by a wide belt, which would have been ornamented with precious stone for ladies at court. The head-dress worn at this time was still the cones of hair on each side of the head, with either a veil or the 'canopy' top as previously described.

To make the Houppelande, choose a simple raglan sleeved dress or coat pattern and adapt it to the layout shown here. As will be seen it has an opening from the V-neck to the waist, this should be fastened with hooks and bar eyes or lacing, and not with a zip unless it can be completely concealed; if zips are permitted to show they strike such a bad note and spoil the period illusion. The gown sloped out from under the arms, and to obtain the necessary width material of at least 48 inches wide should be used; if narrower material is used it must be pieced out at the hem. The raglan sleeves are long and wide at the ends with points, the turn-back should be of contrasting material though fur or fur fabric would be best if they are obtainable. An under-dress was worn with tight sleeves which showed at the wrists, and for this the under-sleeves made to wear with Saxon tunic could be used again, thus saving extra work.

The collar was simple and very modern looking, it was sometimes double, one layer being larger than the other, and made of linen. Later in the reign of Henry VI the sleeves became narrower and were gathered into a band, and with this style went the wide look neck-line often edged with fur, after which the 'gown shape' gave way to the small, tight bodice, high waist and full skirt of 1461. One point about the Houppelande: it is liable to get disarranged in action, particularly if an actress has to lift her hands above shoulder level. Watch for this at the dress rehearsal, for it will cause unsightly blousing above the belt and pull up the skirt especially at the sides. It is safest to sew the belt onto the gown across the back, and to just beyond the side seams, arranging the folds evenly; this must be done on the figure to get the folds in the right place.

Soft, but fairly heavy material is needed, but as this type of dress has a very limited period of wear it would be better economically, if plain or suitably patterned old curtains or bedspreads could be used. The patterns of that period were stylised repetitive designs, not sprays of flowers or stripes (see Illustration 3, p. 21).

Thus ends the era of the gown for several hundred years. Always remember when dressing a play that in any period up until modern times, the elaborate fashions *could* only be worn by ladies of leisure with tire-women to dress them, for not only were fashionable garments too expensive, they were often impossible to work in. So servants and poor people would have worn the simple gown and a wimple with a thick veil over it, and perhaps a plain version of the surcoat which looked more like a full-length apron with a top and back, than the elaborate garment worn by wealthy ladies. This division of classes by the clothes they wore lasted for hundreds of years, and was even controlled by laws during some periods. The working people always wore a simplified version of the current

ILLUSTRATION No 2.

WORKING
WOMEN.

1310

EDWARD II.
1307-27.

1320

HENRY
VI.
1410-

RICHARD II.
1377-99.

ER.

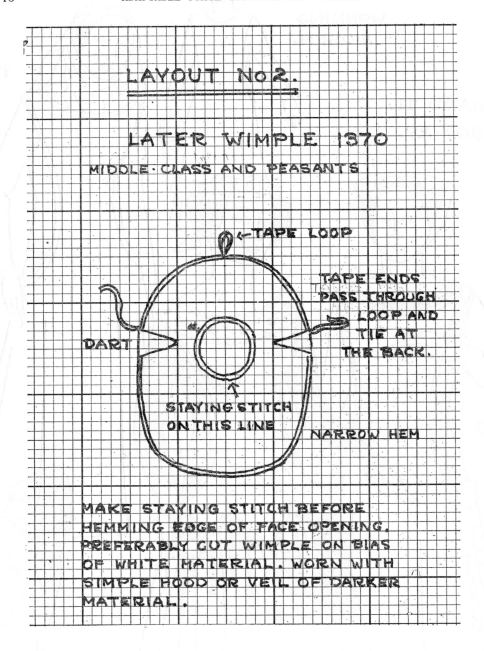

fashion up till the last fifty or sixty years, when modern materials and wholesale methods of production have made it possible for us all to look alike.

Suitable colours for the Fitted Gown. Green, yellow, red, russet, grey and browns. After about 1150 scarlet, a new colour, can be used for additions and cloaks, but only for the nobility.

Shoes (see Diagram 1, p. 11) were flat with a pointed toe, a shape fashionable till about 1969, and still likely to be found at Jumble Sales. If such shoes or

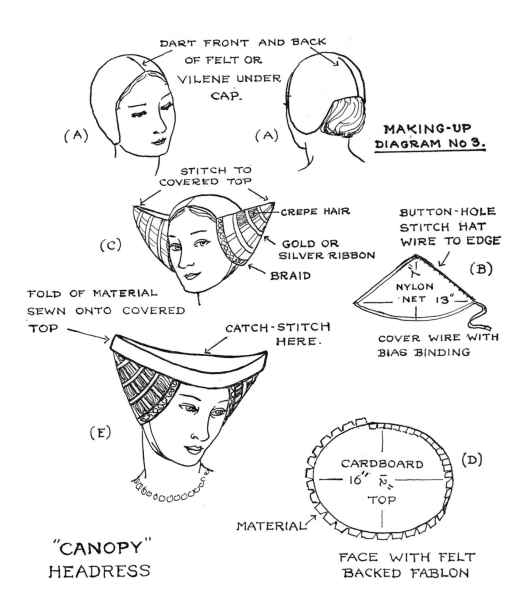

DART FRONT AND BACK OF FELT OR VILENE UNDER CAP.

(A)

(A)

MAKING-UP DIAGRAM NO 3.

STITCH TO COVERED TOP

(C)

CREPE HAIR

GOLD OR SILVER RIBBON

BRAID

BUTTON-HOLE STITCH HAT WIRE TO EDGE

(B)

NYLON NET 13"

COVER WIRE WITH BIAS BINDING

FOLD OF MATERIAL SEWN ONTO COVERED TOP

CATCH-STITCH HERE.

(E)

CARDBOARD 16" 2. TOP

(D)

MATERIAL

"CANOPY" HEADRESS

FACE WITH FELT BACKED FABLON

slippers can't be found, mask a flat shoe with a casing made of Fablon and felt, using two thicknesses of the heaviest weight Fablon for the soles and felt for the tops. Cut the Fablon to the same size as the sole of the shoe but extend the toe to a point. Next make a pattern in paper of the top front part of the shoe, extending the toe to match the sole and allowing a ¾-inch turning on the edge where it will join the sole. Using the pattern, cut out in felt of a suitable colour, clipping the turning. Remove the paper backing from the upper layer of the sole, stick the clipped edge of the felt top over the edge, next remove the backing from the other layer of Fablon and press the two adhesive surfaces together sealing in the clipped turning of the felt top. Pad the pointed toe with cotton wool, slip the masking section over the shoe and fix in place with a strip of Fablon (see Diagram 1E). This shape of shoe remained fashionable till the time of Henry VII, 1485.

PLAYS
The Widow of Heardingas, 1071
Lion in Winter, Henry II, 1154
Becket, 1118–70
Left Handed Liberty, 1199
The Six Wives of Calais, 1347
Richard of Bordeaux, 1385–97
The Lady's not for Burning, 1400
The Boy with a Cart
The Maid of Domremy
The Dream
The Canterbury Tales and one-act adaptations

CHAPTER III

BASIC BODICE AND SKIRT

*H*OW *to make up the Basic bodice and skirt.*

Having cut out *the bodice* according to Layout 3 (on a folded sheet facing p. 32) and marked all darts and stitching lines on the right side of the lining material, the shoulder seams of the dress fabric and the lining are stitched up separately and the seams pressed open (see Diagram 4A, p. 22). Then the right side of the dress fabric is pinned to the right side of the lining and stitched round the armhole, neck and down the back; at this stage the bodice is in two halves, a right half and a left half. Clip round the armhole and neck, especially into the corners of the bodice neckline, then turn right side out by pulling the back section through the shoulder space: you will then have a right and left side of the bodice. Press them well and oversew all raw edges (by machine if possible, any swing needle machine can do this) and stitch matching straight binding to the bottom sections of the bodice (see Diagram 4B). The bodice fabric and the lining are now held together as one, and are sewn as if they were one thickness of material. First sew the darts in place and press them, then the centre front and side seams are sewn on the marked stitching line using a long stitch, number 6 or 8 is recommended (see Diagram 4C). The hem of the bodice is turned up and hemmed in place by hand. Lastly hooks and bar eyes size 3 are sewn down the back opening, the edge of which should be stitched as this prevents the hooks pulling the material out of line, and strengthens the edge (see Diagram 4D). Do not stint on hooks and eyes, there should not be more than $1\frac{1}{2}$ inches between each hook and eye.

The Basic long and below elbow length sleeves are also lined and the notches showing where the sleeve fits the bodice marked with a felt pen on the lining; the bodice lining will have been marked in a like way. All raw edges are oversewn and the bottom of the sleeve finished with straight binding and hemmed up by hand. The top of the sleeves has a row of stitching on the 'ease line' that is gathered up very slightly and a staying row of back-stitch put in by hand on the gathering line; it will then stand up to hard use and wear. Whichever kind of sleeve is used it is first pinned in place, matching the notches (see Diagram 7, p. 29). Then it is sewn in place by hand with a hemming stich, using double thread, with the long stitch under and the short upper stitch just catching in the edge of the bodice armhole. If it has been necessary to let out the underarm seam to fit a large size, the sleeve seam must be let out a corresponding amount.

As all sewing lines and darts are permanently marked, it is easy to adjust for fit and size, and all the seams being oversewn prevents wear and tear. Made this way dresses will last for years in good condition.

Study the 'fitting' Diagram 5, p. 23 and alter the basic dress as the individual figure requires. For instance, with a wide back only the hooks and eyes may need adjusting, while a slightly larger figure will need the front seam let out as well, and for a bigger size all over the side seams and sleeve seams must be let out. Make quite sure that the actress stands naturally and that the bodice rests snugly at the waistline. Particular attention should be paid to the proper fit of the back of the bodice; this is very frequently overlooked with very bad results, such as a bulging back caused by it being too long, which may make the actress look hunchbacked, and even cause the hooks to come undone. If a dress is properly fitted none of this will happen, it will feel secure and comfortable, look right in action and beautiful in repose.

Finally, when fitting a dress ask the actress to move about and make the gestures and movements needed in the part, perhaps reaching up to a high shelf or bending down very low. Even climbing out of a window may be needed, though this is unlikely except in Victorian plays which include an elopement.

Layout 3 (between pp. 32 and 33) also shows how to cut out the skirt.

The skirt is made of two widths of 48 inch wide material and 30 inches of another width, all not less than 1¼ yards in length. Stitch the two 48 wide pieces together using No. 6 or 8 stitch length, leave a 3 inch wide turning. This is the centre front and the wide turning is needed when the seam is undone so that the skirt can be opened over an under skirt as in the Elizabethan, Charles II, William and Mary, Anne, and George II, and III periods. The other two edges are sewn to the 30 inch wide pieces, but to within 8 inches of the top on the right side back, this is for the off-centre opening of the skirt. Make a waistband of 2½ inch wide Petersham or double Vilene, and 6 inches longer than the 27 inches which is the waist measurement for the 36 bust size. Cover with the same material as the basic dress, leave the lower edge unstitched until the skirt has been pleated onto the waistband. Mark the waistband with tacks as shown in the layout, and starting at the centre front pin the skirt in deep pleats onto the Petersham or Vilene, so that the folds lie towards the centre front and make a box pleat at the side seam marking, then the fold of the pleats will again lie toward the centre back finishing in an inverted pleat at the centre back marking (see Diagram 6, p. 27). The opening is made off-centre so that if the waist needs to be let out only the back pleats have to be unpicked, this must always extend beyond the centre inverted pleat so that the skirt fullness can be equalised. It is helpful if this back section is sewn by hand with a back-stitch and double thread, as this while strong, makes it very easy to unpick. When all pleats have been sewn in place, slip-stitch the loose edge of the waistband material onto the skirt stitch line, and sew hooks and bar eyes in position using not less than three.

Here are a few ideas for colours to be used for the *basic* dresses. They have been chosen because they will span the centuries from the fashion point of view and combine well with the various 'additions' that make the change of style, they are also good colours under stage lighting.

Silver Grey and Dove Grey. Avoid greys with too much blue in them as they will look drab.

Russet, Golden Brown, Warm Brown, Apricot.

Yellows. But not citreous yellow as this is an essentially modern fashion colour.

Royal Blue, Deep Royal Blue (this will look almost black on stage). All blues should be tested under stage lighting but as long as they have no tinge of mauve in them you will be safe.

ILLUSTRATION No 3.

HENRY V. 1413-22.

← HOUPPELANDE

BASIC COSTUME
WITH THREE QUARTER
AND LONG SLEEVES.

↑
1461.

ℰℛ.

BASIC BODICE.

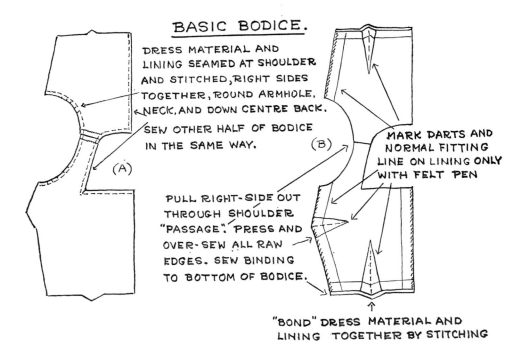

DRESS MATERIAL AND
LINING SEAMED AT SHOULDER
AND STITCHED, RIGHT SIDES
TOGETHER, ROUND ARMHOLE,
NECK, AND DOWN CENTRE BACK.

SEW OTHER HALF OF BODICE
IN THE SAME WAY.

(A)

(B)

PULL RIGHT-SIDE OUT
THROUGH SHOULDER
"PASSAGE". PRESS AND
OVER-SEW ALL RAW
EDGES. SEW BINDING
TO BOTTOM OF BODICE.

MARK DARTS AND
NORMAL FITTING
LINE ON LINING ONLY
WITH FELT PEN

"BOND" DRESS MATERIAL AND
LINING TOGETHER BY STITCHING
DOWN CENTRE OF DARTS

(C)

MAKING-UP DIAGRAM No 4.

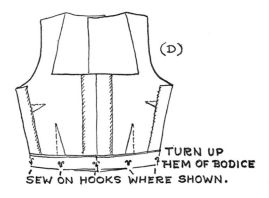

(D)

STITCH DARTS AND SEAMS ON
MARKED LINES, OR AS NEEDED
TO FIT FIGURE. (No 8 STITCH)
BODICE HEM CAN BE TURNED
DOWN TO A POINT IF REQUIRED.

TURN UP
HEM OF BODICE
SEW ON HOOKS WHERE SHOWN.

MAKING·UP DIAGRAM. No 5.

·METHODS of ADJUSTMENT for SIZE and SHAPE.

ALL BODICES MUST FIT TIGHTLY.

(A)

ADJUSTMENT FOR LARGER
TALLER PERSON.
LET OUT ON SIDE, CENTRE
FRONT SEAMS. MOVE "EYES"
AT CENTRE BACK, AND FOR
A TALLER PERSON LET DOWN
BOTTOM HEM OF BODICE. A
½ INCH ON ALL SEAMS AND AT
BACK, ADDS 4" INCHES TO SIZE.

BIG BUST, BASIC SIZE BACK.

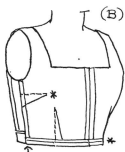

(B)

LET OUT FRONT OF SIDE SEAM
AND CENTRE FRONT SEAM.
INCREASE SIZE OF SIDE DART, *
AND ADJUST FRONT DARTS
TO FIT AT WAIST. LET DOWN *
BODICE FRONT HEM, EQUALIZE
AT SIDE SEAMS.

ROUNDED SHOULDERS
AND/OR BROAD BACK.

DARTS

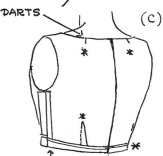

(C)

LET OUT BACK OF SIDE
SEAM. SHORTEN DART *
ADJUST "EYES", CURVE
DOWN HEM *. IF BACK IS
VERY ROUNDED MAKE
SMALL DART IN NECK-
LINE *.

Blackberry. This is a reddish shade of purple.

Purple, Rose Pink, and all shades of *Green* except lime which again is a modern fashion colour.

Variations of these main suggestions may be used provided that they are first tested under stage lighting, a small pattern is not enough; an ⅛ of a yard should be bought and if the reason is explained, few shops will object to the smallness of the amount bought. The most surprising thing is the complete change of effect that the colours of the various additions make to the Basic dress, quite apart from the change in style. Imagine grey allied to black or purple, then think of it with rose pink or apricot and you will get some idea of possible transformations. Suggestions for the correct colour link-ups and additions will be given for each period.

One big don't. Crimson was considered a Royal colour during many periods, so it is a mistake to have it for a Basic dress, it can be added where a Royal person's dress is needed.

CHAPTER IV

VARIATIONS

Variation No. 1. 1461–85. Edward IV and V. Richard III. Wars of the Roses

THE characteristic fashion of this time was the high waist line, wide V neck, deep belts, and skirts rising at the front to rest on top of the foot and dipping at the back to trail a little on the ground.

The change is made by wearing the skirt over the bodice and raising it a little at the centre front to give the upward curve fashionable at this time (see Illustration 3, p. 21 and Diagram 7, p. 29). The hooks must now be placed on the *inside* of the waistband, and the bar eyes sewn on at the centre front, side seams and on all darts. A broad slightly shaped waistband is made in heavyweight Vilene; it should be fitted to rest from the bottom of the skirt waistband upwards, thus giving the effect of a small bodice; it can be covered with material contrasting with the basic dress. A wide collar-like addition ending at the waist is also made of Vilene and can be covered with the same material as the waistband, but contrasting material or fur can be used. Sometimes only a narrow strip of fur was stitched to the outer edge, and the deep V neck was filled in with folds of fine linen. For a rich court dress the waistband can be sewn with 'jewels'. For the sleeves use the long basic sleeve and add a curved section in matching material to extend over the hands (see Layout 4, p. 26). The hem of the skirt should be turned up till it rests on top of the foot, and turned down at the back till it trails a little on the ground.

The *high pointed head-dress* fashionable at this time, is best worn with the softening veil as otherwise the hair will have to be made to look as if it has been shaved back, a most unbecoming effect. Even if this is not done the hard line of the head-dress can only be worn successfully by somebody with youth and very good features to help her. The veil is made of fine voile or nylon material 36 or 45 inches wide. One corner of the square of material is rounded off so that the curved edge just shows beyond the head-dress. The veil must be oversewn all round, and is pinned onto the head, the head-dress being placed over it at a backward slanting angle. A further piece of nylon or voile should be attached to the top of the head-dress and to the lower point of the veil to form a graceful long loop (see Illustration 3, p. 21). Nylon millinery net in double thickness (name of the firm where this can be bought will be found on p. viii) is used to make this head-dress as it is both very stiff yet light. It is covered with lightweight patterned material cut larger than the size of the nylon net; it will thus be able to face back the top and bottom of the head-dress. All three layers of material are bonded together by rows of machine stitching, preferably crosswise to form diamond shapes. If plain and not patterned material is used to cover the head-dress these stitch lines can be painted over with gold or silver paint, and a 'jewel' sewn in the diamond formed by the stitching. Lastly the head-dress is sewn together at the centre back down to the bottom 2 inches, where black or brown elastic is inserted, this helps hold the head-dress firmly on the head, though owing to the slant at which it has to be worn, small hat-pins with matching nobs will probably be needed as well. The bottom was often trimmed with an ornamental band about an inch wide, this can be made of furnishing braid painted in gold or silver (see Diagram 6, p. 27). The amount of 'jewels' and ornamentation will vary with the social status of the part being dressed. Red, Blue or Green sequins are very effective as 'jewels' but do remember, that though diamonds were known to the ancient world and came from India, they were both very rare, and worn only by Kings. Faceting was not

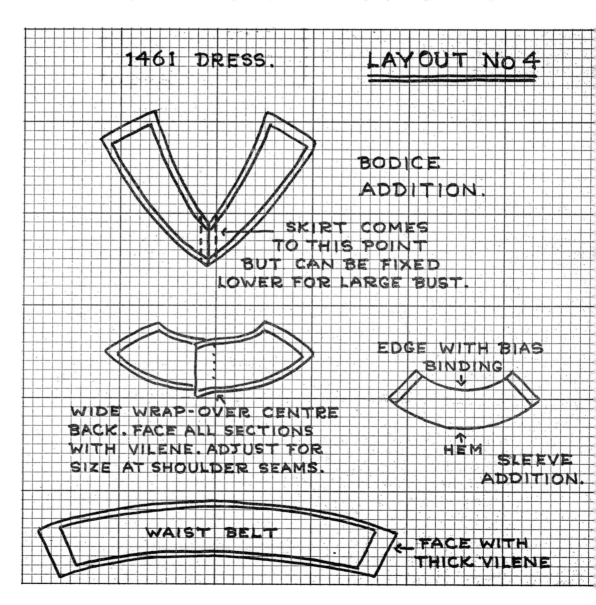

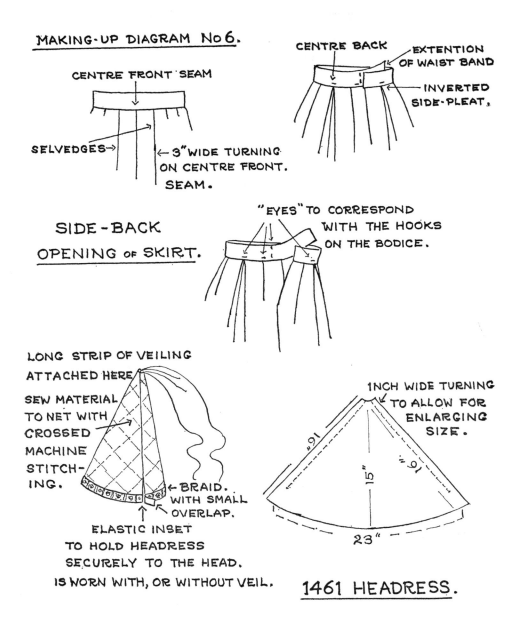

MAKING-UP DIAGRAM No 6.

CENTRE FRONT SEAM

SELVEDGES→

← 3"WIDE TURNING
ON CENTRE FRONT.
SEAM.

CENTRE BACK

EXTENTION
OF WAIST BAND

INVERTED
SIDE-PLEAT,

SIDE-BACK
OPENING of SKIRT.

"EYES" TO CORRESPOND
WITH THE HOOKS
ON THE BODICE.

LONG STRIP OF VEILING
ATTACHED HERE

SEW MATERIAL
TO NET WITH
CROSSED
MACHINE
STITCH-
ING.

← BRAID.
WITH SMALL
OVERLAP.

ELASTIC INSET
TO HOLD HEADRESS
SECURELY TO THE HEAD.
IS WORN WITH, OR WITHOUT VEIL.

1 INCH WIDE TURNING
TO ALLOW FOR
ENLARGING
SIZE.

16"

16"

15"

23"

1461 HEADRESS.

yet practised as we know it today; it was not until the middle of the eighteenth century that diamonds were cut so that they became the brilliant glittering stones we know today.

Collar-like necklaces were worn at this time, and these can be made of gold or silver lace gathered along the straight edge to fit the neck and lie flat round the throat. The other edge should be of a pointed design and pearls or coloured glass shapes stitched onto suitable parts of the design. Rings can always be made of coloured glass beads and gold or silver wire (fuse wire if silver is required) or a strip of cardboard covered with gold or silver paper, onto which some beads can be stitched. Many fancy goods shops sell flat coloured stones which have small holes at the edges so that they are very easy to sew anywhere they are needed. Suggestion for colours and materials.

Colour of Dress		Additions
Blackberry	x	Wine red in plain material or velvet.
		Gold or Silver tissue (Royalty only).
Purple	x	Sky blue or golden yellow plain material or patterned.
Royal Blue	x	Gold coloured material plain or patterned, and/or fur, or fur fabric.
Greens	x	Darker green velvet or gold tissue.
		Patterned material in russet shades.
Russet	x	Purple material patterned or plain.
		Dark brown velvet.
Sky Blue	x	Patterned material in gold or silver.
		Brown fur with gold coloured belt.

This is not a period rich in plays, though for any play about the Wars of the Roses, Richard III, or the Princes in the Tower, this would be the right costume of the period. It is also the almost traditional dress for the Fairy-Tale Princess, not to mention the Wicked Stepmother of the same tales.

Variation No. 2.   Henry VII, 1485–1509. Henry VIII, 1509–47
(see Illustration 4, p. 31)

The fashions during the first Tudor reign were very simple in style, possibly the reflection of a miserly King. Many of the dresses and habits worn by nuns until quite recently are a direct inheritance from this period; the head-dress and veil certainly were.

A fitted bodice now ended at the natural waist-line, with a narrow sash, and the neck was filled in over the shoulder usually with contrasting material. For this velvet could be used, and also for facing back the long, wide-ended sleeves; but fur was often used to face the sleeves, though not the neck, but both velvet and fur would only have been worn by well-to-do people (see Diagram 8, p. 33 for shoulder section and sleeve).

The *hood*, which was the name given to the head-dress worn at this time, was sometimes rounded, but the English 'gable' shape was more popular and is

MAKING-UP DIAGRAM No 7.

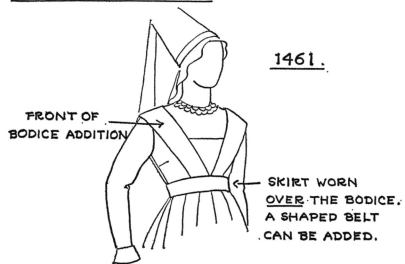

1461.

FRONT OF
BODICE ADDITION

SKIRT WORN
OVER THE BODICE.
A SHAPED BELT
CAN BE ADDED.

BACK SECTION OF
BODICE ADDITION.

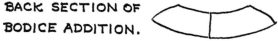

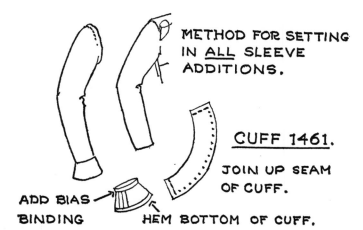

METHOD FOR SETTING
IN ALL SLEEVE
ADDITIONS.

CUFF 1461.

JOIN UP SEAM
OF CUFF.

ADD BIAS
BINDING

HEM BOTTOM OF CUFF.

typical of this period in its simpler form, and it was still worn for the first twenty years of the reign of Henry VIII, being the favourite head wear of Catherine of Aragon (see Layout 5, p. 36 for gable hoods, and Diagrams 9 and 10, pp. 35, 37 for making both kinds). To make the under-cap worn with the gable hoods: using the shape shown in the layout, cut it out in two layers of white millinery nylon net and one layer of white cotton material. Stitch in the dart at the centre top, sewing the two layers of nylon net as if one thickness of material. Pin the cotton and nylon together and machine with a fine stitch (No. 12) round the front edge and sides, turn right side out and press. Then fit into the front edge and sides white hat wire, turning back the ends, stitch in place by hand or machine and firm the ends of the wire with several strong stitches using double thread and hand sewing. Next make the dart in the centre of the back section and bind the bottom with white bias binding. Pin the back section to front with the cotton covered side next to the face, and the raw edge of the turning on the upper side. Stitch together with a fine stitch. Sew a piece of ribbon at the point where the cap touches the bottom of the ear, this is pinned in place at the same point on the other side when the cap is worn. In this instance pinning is better and more secure than hooks and eyes. Cut a piece of ornamental material about 13 inches long and 5 inches wide, make this into a roll with cotton wool, turning in the ends and raw edges. Make a slight dart centre front to match the point of the cap, sew the roll to the cap at the side angle points and the centre front. Next make the 'hood' part which was usually made in some dark coloured material: cut out to the same shape as the under-cap, but allow two more inches on the front edge. At the same time cut a lining of two layers of black millinery nylon net, but this is only the size of the cap. Face back the extra 2 inches of the 'hood' material with brightly patterned or plain material, stitch, turn right side out and press.

At this point the making of the Henry VII Gable hood and the Henry VIII gable varies. For the Henry VII version the sides of the hood are cut longer and hung down 8 to 12 inches beyond the under cap. It was made exactly as the under-cap was made, but the back section should be cut a little larger all round, and wired to maintain the shape. Turn over the ends of the wire and use long button-hole stitches to hold it in place. Cut a matching piece of material the same shape at the top as the back of the hood, but widening out at the bottom; it should be about 22 inches long and hang loose like a veil, and be stitched to the hood along the top back part. For the Henry VIII version the hood must be stitched round the back and sides, turn right side out and press, then insert a piece of black hat wire along the *back* seam, and stitch into place. Tack the raw edges of the nylon net and the coloured facing into place, trimming them so that they just meet then stitch a piece of binding over the joining point to hold them in place and make it neat. The back of the hood is made by cutting two lengths of material and two lengths of black millinery nylon net 7 inches wide and about 28 inches long; the length varied, some women preferred shorter 'ends'. Stitch the net and material together $\frac{1}{2}$ inch in from the edge round the two long and one of the short ends, turn right side out and press, then slip-stitch together the other end. With an over-sewing stitch sew one of the ends from the centre back of the hood down the left side, bending the wire when the short edge is finished and continuing to the end of the side of the hood on the long part of the 'ends'. Then stitch the short end of the other length to the right

HENRY VII. 1485 - 1509.

1485.

HENRY VIII. 1509 -47.

1530.

1541.

ILLUSTRATION NO 4.

side of the hood, again starting at the centre top. The 'ends' are then crossed over to form the square effect, and where the edge of the square meets the hood on the right side both layers are held to the bottom of the hood with a few very strong stitches. This also applies where the long 'end' that folds to the left is in line with the bottom of the hood on that side. The bottom point of square must also be stitched firmly. The hood is then placed over the under-cap and pinned into position with colour headed pin which should match the material, first at the top centre front and then over the ears at the point where the chinstrap is sewn to the under-cap. Owing to the lightness and strength of the stiffening materials used this head-dress is not the top-heavy horror it could otherwise be, in fact I wear one when giving my demonstration (see Diagram 9B, p. 35).

Suitable colours. Russet, Brown, Greens, Blue-Green, Grey, with some red, especially a deep claret red for additions.

Jewellery was very simple, a shortish chain necklace and an occasional ring. People did not display their wealth in case the King decided that they could therefore pay higher taxes.

PLAYS

Not many have as yet been written about the reign of Henry VII but the present general interest in the Tudors may well spark off an interest in him and his times.

When Henry VIII came to the throne, clothes, especially for men, became very extravagant, but the women's dresses still had much the same line as in the previous reign, though the sleeves and head-dresses became more elaborate. Several different neck-lines were fashionable: one was low and square with an edging of ruched lace or linen, others were filled in with contrasting material stitched to the dress and ended in a pretty face framing collar; another style looked very like a brief bolero and was worn over the dress with the filled in neck of gathered linen showing at the throat in a frilled stand-up collar (see Layout 6, p. 42 for fill-in, collar, and 'bolero'). Middle-class women wore their dresses higher at the neck and filled in after the manner of the previous reign.

The style of the sleeves changed very much between the early and the latter parts of the reign. With the gable hoods big folds of drapery hung from just above the elbow and were worn with an under sleeve gathered and frilled at the wrist. It is surprisingly easy to make this version, using material such as brocade, velvet or fur fabric cut to the shape and size shown in the layout for sleeves of this period (see Diagram 11, p. 39). Stitch up the curved end and round the sides to within the width of the basic below elbow sleeve, then sew the drapery onto the main sleeve about two inches above the elbow and stitch the other opening to the bottom edge of the sleeve; pin into large folds and stitch to the upper side of the main sleeve using four or five cross-stitches in matching thread. Next make the under-sleeve, this too is very easy and can be used under one of the later 'bell' sleeves. Use 24 inches of 36 inch wide cotton material or taffeta for rich people, cut in two along the fold line, turn over the selvedges to a narrow hem and edge stitch; a little lace can be added at the same time, but only for rich people. Hem together the 18 inch sides, turn over then to make a hem wide enough to take a narrow piece of elastic, to fit the size of the upper arm. Lastly stitch a strip of bias binding round the under-sleeve 1¼ inches up from

HENRY VII. ADDITIONS.

MAKING-UP DIAGRAM No 8.

1485—

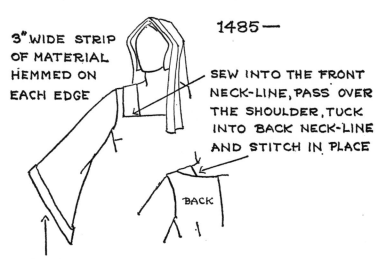

3" WIDE STRIP
OF MATERIAL
HEMMED ON
EACH EDGE

SEW INTO THE FRONT
NECK-LINE, PASS OVER
THE SHOULDER, TUCK
INTO BACK NECK-LINE
AND STITCH IN PLACE

BACK

FUR, OR FOLD
OF MATERIAL TO
MATCH NECK FILLING.

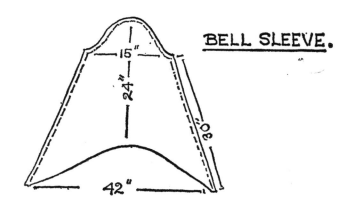

BELL SLEEVE.

15"

24"

30"

42"

the selvedge on the wrong side of the material, through this run a length of elastic to fit the wrist. You will then have a full sleeve with a frilled end, it should be put on before the dress, then puffed out to show below the main sleeve. The two 'bells' are the same shape but the one worn with the ornate undersleeve is slightly shorter. They must be lined throughout; old sheeting can be used, and faced back at the bottom for not less than 4 inches, otherwise the lining would show. They are sewn to the basic below elbow sleeve just above the elbow, then 1½ inches of the sleeve is allowed to fold upwards, thereby standing a little away from the arm; this is caught in place with a few strong stitches, but not sewn all the way round. The ornate under-sleeve is a variation of the one previously described. It can be made of striped material or strips of velvet and brocade each about 2 inches wide, stitched together to make up to about the same width and length as given for the previous under-sleeve. The sleeve is finished with a narrow band. It can be used again with the 'cuff' sleeve of Mary Tudor (Mary I).

Anne Bullen (or Boleyn as they later spelt their name) who had lived much at the French court is said to have introduced the *French Hood*, which was very attractive, and less fantastic in shape than some of the gable hoods had become. Hair was no longer braided to support the gable hood, but was parted in the centre and brushed smoothly down (see Illustration 4, p. 31). The basic difference between the French and the English hood was the round shaped back of the former and the squared out front and top of the back section of the latter (see Diagram 12, p. 41). The front section of the French hood was also less deep and the hair was shown more. All hoods were worn over an under cap, but it is not necessary to make one as the frilled edge was all that showed, and this can be simulated by pleating white material or crêpe paper onto the inside edge of the hood. A piece of matching material about 21 inches in length, hung from the back of the hood. This can be of double thickness if the hood is made of fairly thin material; it should be sewn to the hood along the join of the front and back sections. It falls more gracefully if it is cut a little wider at the bottom than the top. A variation of the English hood had a rounded back section and the squared front angle was softened to a curve and dipped in the centre front. All these hoods are made up by exactly the same method as used to make the undercap for the gable hood, the only difference in method is that hat wire should also be sewn along the join of the back and front section, using long button-hole stitches. This wiring makes it easy to shape line of the hood as is required. The hoods still tended to be made in dark colours of velvet or silk material, with various kinds of ornamentation such as bands of contrasting material, gold or silver braid, and sometimes a padded roll of material where the front and back joined (see Layout 5, p. 36). Women trimmed their hoods as our mothers trimmed their hats, and so long as the correct basic line is adhered to, and an indication of an under-cap shown, all sorts of variations on the main theme can be achieved. This prevents all the actresses looking alike, which is never a good thing apart from a Musical Comedy chorus!

Suitable Colours. Russet and tawny shades, greens, light and dark, blue, blackberry, apricot, grey. For Royalty and Nobility only: deep crimson and blue velvet.

Jewellery. This was still rather simple. Chains were worn round the neck on which a medallion or locket-like ornament was hung. Belts were very ornamental

UNDER CAP AND GABLE HOOD.

MAKING-UP DIAGRAM No 9.

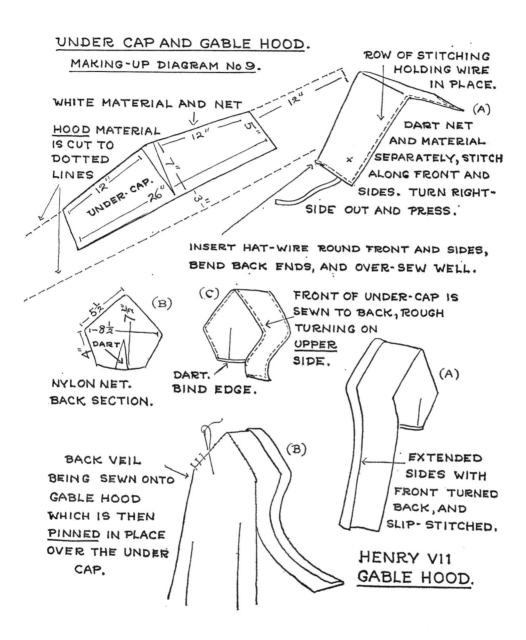

WHITE MATERIAL AND NET

HOOD MATERIAL IS CUT TO DOTTED LINES

12"

12"

5"

7"

UNDER CAP.

12"

26"

3"

ROW OF STITCHING HOLDING WIRE IN PLACE.

(A)

DART NET AND MATERIAL SEPARATELY, STITCH ALONG FRONT AND SIDES. TURN RIGHT-SIDE OUT AND PRESS.

×

INSERT HAT-WIRE ROUND FRONT AND SIDES, BEND BACK ENDS, AND OVER-SEW WELL.

$5\frac{1}{2}$

$\frac{1}{2}$

$7\frac{1}{2}$

$1-8\frac{1}{2}$

DART

(B)

NYLON NET. BACK SECTION.

(C)

DART. BIND EDGE.

FRONT OF UNDER-CAP IS SEWN TO BACK, ROUGH TURNING ON UPPER SIDE.

(A)

(B)

BACK VEIL BEING SEWN ONTO GABLE HOOD WHICH IS THEN PINNED IN PLACE OVER THE UNDER CAP.

EXTENDED SIDES WITH FRONT TURNED BACK, AND SLIP-STITCHED.

HENRY V11 GABLE HOOD.

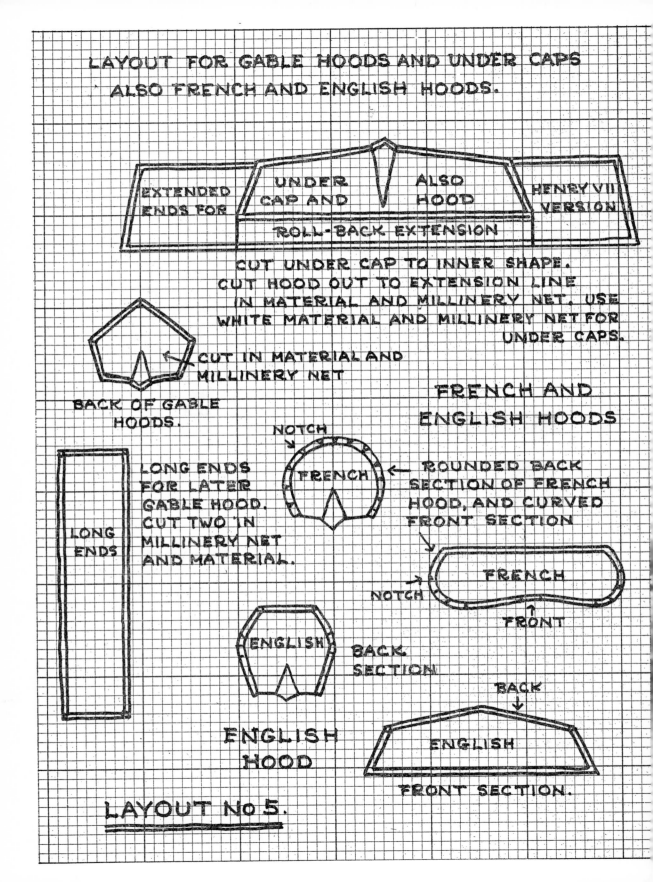

LAYOUT FOR GABLE HOODS AND UNDER CAPS
ALSO FRENCH AND ENGLISH HOODS.

EXTENDED ENDS FOR

UNDER CAP AND

ALSO HOOD

HENRY VII VERSION

ROLL-BACK EXTENSION

CUT UNDER CAP TO INNER SHAPE.
CUT HOOD OUT TO EXTENSION LINE
IN MATERIAL AND MILLINERY NET. USE
WHITE MATERIAL AND MILLINERY NET FOR
UNDER CAPS.

CUT IN MATERIAL AND
MILLINERY NET

BACK OF GABLE HOODS.

FRENCH AND ENGLISH HOODS

NOTCH

FRENCH

ROUNDED BACK SECTION OF FRENCH HOOD, AND CURVED FRONT SECTION

LONG ENDS FOR LATER GABLE HOOD. CUT TWO IN MILLINERY NET AND MATERIAL.

LONG ENDS

FRENCH

NOTCH

FRONT

ENGLISH

BACK SECTION

ENGLISH HOOD

BACK

ENGLISH

FRONT SECTION.

LAYOUT No 5.

GABLE HOOD. HENRY VIII.

MAKING-UP DIAGRAM No 10.

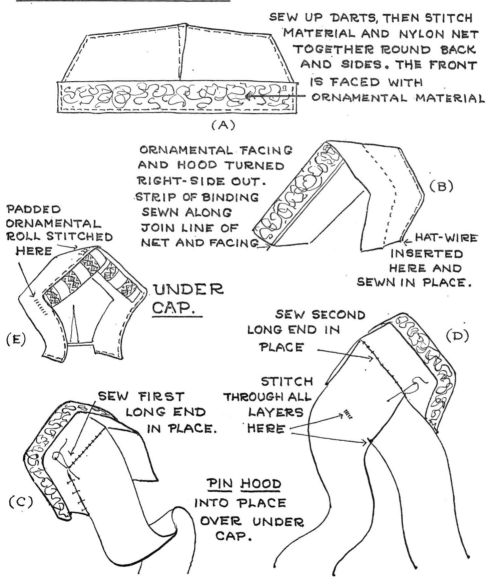

SEW UP DARTS, THEN STITCH MATERIAL AND NYLON NET TOGETHER ROUND BACK AND SIDES. THE FRONT IS FACED WITH ORNAMENTAL MATERIAL

(A)

ORNAMENTAL FACING AND HOOD TURNED RIGHT-SIDE OUT. STRIP OF BINDING SEWN ALONG JOIN LINE OF NET AND FACING

(B)

HAT-WIRE INSERTED HERE AND SEWN IN PLACE.

PADDED ORNAMENTAL ROLL STITCHED HERE

UNDER CAP.

(E)

SEW SECOND LONG END IN PLACE

(D)

STITCH THROUGH ALL LAYERS HERE

SEW FIRST LONG END IN PLACE.

PIN HOOD INTO PLACE OVER UNDER CAP.

(C)

and stitched with precious stones. Furnishing braid painted gold or silver is very good for this purpose, in the early part of the reign a cross often hung from the end of the belt, later the belts were very simple.

PLAYS

Henry VIII and his six wives have been an endless source of material for plays of all kinds. Of the many a few.

A Man for all Seasons
Rose without a Thorn
Royal Gambit

Variation No. 3 Edward VI, 1547–53, and Mary I (Mary Tudor), 1553–58

The clothes fashionable during the reigns of the two female Tudors were as different as their characters. In Mary's time the dress was rich but simple with high necks and collars, inside of which small ruffs were sometimes worn, filling the neckline up to the chin. The bodice was longer and to achieve this effect a roll of material, cut on the cross and banded with a contrasting colour, is stitched to the edge of the bodice and set from the waist downwards like a girdle, a long end of which should hang down to the level of the hem, with an ornament, such as a golden ball at its end. This ornament can be made by painting a very small ball with gold paint, or covering one with gold material, a few beads can be added for jewels. To add to the long bodice look, a matching piece of material should be used to fill in the neck and cover the shoulders of the basic dress; slip-stitch this into place as the join should show as little as possible; if masking is necessary use a narrow matching braid. Use the same layout as was used for the contrasting fill-in for Henry VIII dress, cutting the separate collar to the longer points as shown by the dotted line (see Layout 6, p. 42 and Diagram 13, p. 43). There is another layout for the collar cut in one with the bodice version, this collar is usually faced with contrasting material. The extended shoulder piece became fashionable and often matched the collar facing and/or the cuff. It is made by cutting 4 melon shaped pieces of material to span from the back notches of the sleeve to the front ones. Stitch the outer curves together inter facing with medium weight Vilene, stitch by hand to the top of the sleeve. If the simple version is used the basic long sleeve with a small cuff and narrow frill will be suitable. For the 'cuffed' sleeve shown in Illustration 5 the basic below elbow sleeve will be required. Cut out in buckram the semi-circular shape shown in Layout 6, p. 42, cover the inside with material sticking it into place with Copydex. Lap over the buckram at the join to fit the bottom of the sleeve. Cut a strip of material 5 inches wide, and long enough to go round the upper edge of the buckram. Tack this to the inside and the ornamental material to the outside of the buckram, sew round by hand with double thread. Fold back the material and sew the lower curve of the buckram to the bottom of the sleeve, again by hand. Gather the ornamental material into a narrow band, to which an edging of lace can be added for rich people (see Diagram 14, p. 44).

The skirt was sometimes opened down the centre front to show a small width

SLEEVES 1530 – 1541 –
MAKING-UP DIAGRAM No 11.

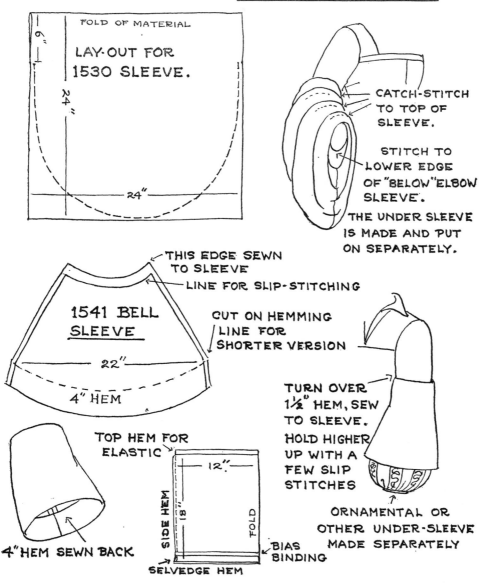

FOLD OF MATERIAL

6"

LAY-OUT FOR
1530 SLEEVE.

24"

24"

CATCH-STITCH
TO TOP OF
SLEEVE.

STITCH TO
LOWER EDGE
OF "BELOW" ELBOW
SLEEVE.
THE UNDER SLEEVE
IS MADE AND PUT
ON SEPARATELY.

THIS EDGE SEWN
TO SLEEVE
LINE FOR SLIP-STITCHING

1541 BELL
SLEEVE

CUT ON HEMMING
LINE FOR
SHORTER VERSION

22"

4" HEM

TURN OVER
1½" HEM, SEW
TO SLEEVE.
HOLD HIGHER
UP WITH A
FEW SLIP
STITCHES

TOP HEM FOR
ELASTIC

12"

SIDE HEM   18"   FOLD

4" HEM SEWN BACK

SELVEDGE HEM

BIAS
BINDING

ORNAMENTAL OR
OTHER UNDER-SLEEVE
MADE SEPARATELY

of underskirt; this was often in plain material but contrasting colour, or just a darker shade of the basic dress, and for very rich people it might be made of brocade. The hood style remained much as before, the centre 'dip' was fashionable and the padded roll of material along the join line of the front and back section, equally so.

Suitable colours. Blackberry (purple), greens, russet, blues, blue-green a little grey, deep rose red for trimmings.

PLAYS

Not very many, though more may be written now that there is so much interest in the Tudors.

The Young Elizabeth

Variation No. 4   Elizabeth I, 1558–1603

It is interesting to note that at sometime in their youth Henry VIII, Elizabeth I, and Charles II were all, for various reasons, kept short of money, and the latter two even of clothes, and in each case when they came to the throne the fashions became very extravagant. Elizabeth set the example of rich clothes for women, but it should be borne in mind when dressing a play of this period, that no Lady-in-Waiting would have been rash enough to vie with her in richness of dress.

The *ruff* introduced in the last reign now became very fashionable in various sizes very much according to social importance; there were even laws about the size that could be worn: the larger and richer the ruff the more important the person. These are best made of the stiff kind of plastic tablecloth, using the lace edged part for the richer ruffs, or of paper taffeta which was used for petticoats a few years ago and may still be found at Jumble Sales. Both these materials remain stiff when washed and need no starching. A neck band of cotton material doubled to finish $1\frac{1}{2}$ to 2 inches wide, is made to fit an average neck and hooked up at the back, a dart must be made at the centre front so that the band lies comfortably round the neck and does not ride up. The plastic or paper taffeta is then cut in strips 3 to 5 inches wide according to the social importance of the character who is wearing the ruff, and stitched by hand in a zig-zag up and down the neck band. It is not a quick job but one that can be picked up at any time, and so gets done quite painlessly! (see Diagram 15, p. 45). A form of ruff was worn at the top of the skirt and looked very like a farthingale, though it is much easier to wear, not having the awkward tendency to tip up when the actress sits down. This is made by cutting two long strips of material that match or complement the colours of the dress, about 13 inches wide and facing them with millinery nylon net to within one box-pleat of the point at which the 'ruff' will go under the stomacher, as here it must lie flat and not stick out. Fold the materials over and press so that you have a strip about $6\frac{1}{2}$ inches wide, this is box-pleated and stitched by hand to the top of the skirt with the turning underneath. At the back, fold the ends into a box pleat to correspond with the skirt opening. In the centre front, keep the 'ruff' flat so that the stomacher will lie over it smoothly. The ends should overlap and be tacked together. (See Illustration 5, p. 47).

FRENCH HOOD.

←NOTCH

CUT TWO LAYERS OF BLACK
NYLON NET, STITCH TO
MATERIAL ALONG SIDES
AND FRONT.

MAKING-UP DIAGRAM No 12.

TURN RIGHT-SIDE OUT AND
INSERT HAT-WIRE ROUND FRONT
AND SIDES. STITCH IN PLACE.

(A) ← PIN RIGHT SIDES
OF FRONT AND
BACK TOGETHER.
SEW BY HAND WITH
BACK-STITCHES.

DART BACK
SECTION THROUGH ALL
LAYERS OF MATERIAL.
BIND BOTTOM EDGE.

USING WELL SPACED
BUTTON-HOLE,
STITCH HAT-WIRE TO
JOIN LINE. BEND BACK
ENDS, OVERSEW.

(B)

(C)

SEW CHIN
STRAP INTO
PLACE

TURN CAP RIGHT-SIDE
OUT CAREFULLY.
SEW A PLEATED
EDGING OF MATERIAL
OR CREPE PAPER TO
THE INSIDE EDGE.

TRIM WITH VELVET OR BRAID.

ENGLISH HOOD.

CHIN
STRAP

2" WIDE BAND
OF WHITE MATERIAL
WITH LACE OR PLEATED
EDGE. SEW AT CENTRE
TOP AND SIDES TO FIT
ROUND FACE.

(D)

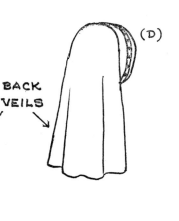

CUT TOP OF
VEIL TO MATCH
SHAPE OF HOOD

BACK
VEILS

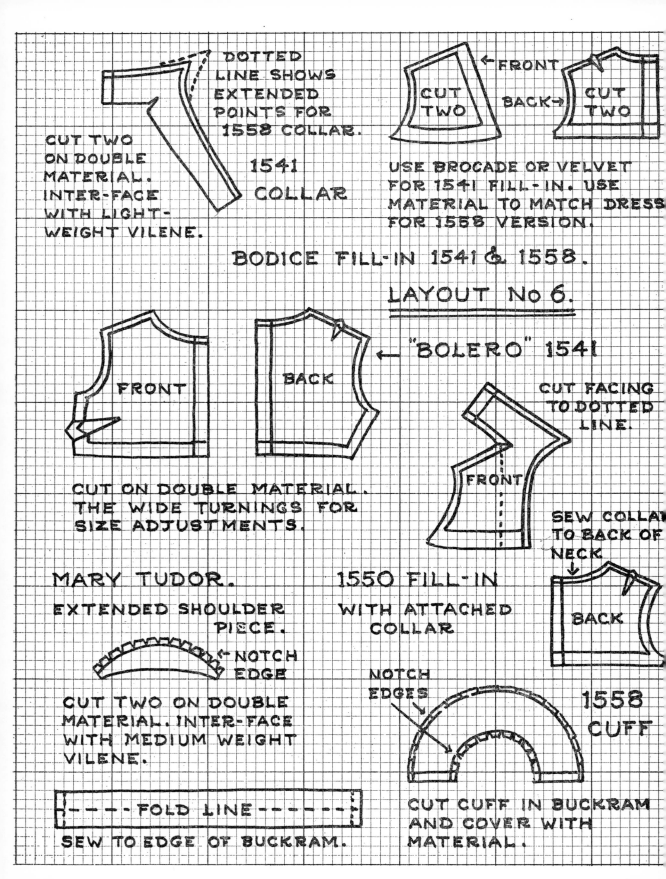

DOTTED LINE SHOWS EXTENDED POINTS FOR 1558 COLLAR.

1541 COLLAR

CUT TWO ON DOUBLE MATERIAL. INTER-FACE WITH LIGHT-WEIGHT VILENE.

← FRONT

CUT TWO

BACK →

CUT TWO

USE BROCADE OR VELVET FOR 1541 FILL-IN. USE MATERIAL TO MATCH DRESS FOR 1558 VERSION.

BODICE FILL-IN 1541 & 1558.

LAYOUT No 6.

← "BOLERO" 1541

FRONT

BACK

CUT ON DOUBLE MATERIAL. THE WIDE TURNINGS FOR SIZE ADJUSTMENTS.

CUT FACING TO DOTTED LINE.

FRONT

SEW COLLAR TO BACK OF NECK

BACK

MARY TUDOR.

EXTENDED SHOULDER PIECE.

← NOTCH EDGE

CUT TWO ON DOUBLE MATERIAL. INTER-FACE WITH MEDIUM WEIGHT VILENE.

1550 FILL-IN

WITH ATTACHED COLLAR

NOTCH EDGES

1558 CUFF

- - - FOLD LINE - - - -

SEW TO EDGE OF BUCKRAM.

CUT CUFF IN BUCKRAM AND COVER WITH MATERIAL.

ADDITIONS. 1541-58

MAKING-UP DIAGRAM No 13.

FACE BACK OF NECK
WITH BIAS BINDING.

(A)

WIDE TURNINGS FOR
SIZE ADJUSTMENTS.

1541 —

(B) EDGES TURNED
OVER, AND FILL-IN
SLIP-STITCHED
INTO PLACE.
THE SAME FILL
-IN IS USED
FOR THE 1550
VERSION, BUT THEN
MATERIAL TO MATCH THE
DRESS MUST BE USED.

MAKE IN
THIN WHITE
MATERIAL.
BIND INSIDE
EDGES. COLLAR IS PUT
ON SEPARATELY. TACK IN
PLACE ON LEFT SIDE, HOLD
WITH SAFETY-PINS ON RIGHT.

DOTTED
LINE MARKS
1558 VERSION

COLLAR-IN-ONE FILL-IN
1550-58

NOTCH →

(A)

SEW-UP SHOULDER
SEAMS AND CENTRE
BACK OF COLLAR.
SEW FACING AND
INTER-FACING
TO RIGHT SIDE
OF COLLAR. TURN
RIGHT-SIDE OUT
AND PRESS.

"BOLERO" 1541 —

FACE EDGE OF NECK AND
ARM-HOLE
WITH BIAS
BINDING.

SEW COLLAR TO BACK OF FILL-IN,
NOTCH NECK EDGE, NEATEN BY
(B) FACING WITH
BIAS BINDING.

1553 SLEEVE

NOTCH EDGE.

(A) COVER BUCKRAM ON INSIDE WITH MATERIAL. OVER-LAP JOIN TO FIT BOTTOM OF SLEEVE.

(B) TACK ORNAMENTAL SLEEVE SECTION TO OUTSIDE OF BUCKRAM, AND BAND TO INSIDE. SEW TOGETHER BY HAND, WITH BACK-STITCH.

(C) ROLL BACK ORNAMENTAL MATERIAL AND SEW BUCKRAM TO BOTTOM OF SLEEVE.

(D) GATHER BOTTOM OF ORNAMENTAL MATERIAL INTO NARROW BAND TO FIT WRIST.

1580 SLEEVE.

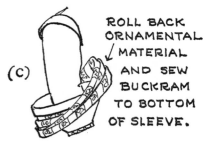

(A) SEW INSET STRIP TO BACK AND FRONT SLEEVE SECTIONS.

(B) MAKE INVERTED PLEAT OF INSET AT TOP AND BOTTOM OF SLEEVE. SEW IN PLACE, AND CATCH SLEEVE EDGES TOGETHER WITH PEARLS OR "JEWELLED" BUTTONS. ADD FRILL.

(C) ORNAMENT AND PAD "EPAULET" OR SHOULDER PIECE. SEW BY HAND TO SLEEVE.

MAKING-UP DIAGRAM No 14.

RUFFS AND FILL-IN   MAKING-UP DIAGRAM No 15.

CUT BAND IN WHITE MATERIAL 16" LONG
2½" WIDE FOR 1550 RUFF, 4½" WIDE FOR
ELIZABETHAN RUFFS. DART AT CENTRE
FRONT. SEW FILL-IN TO
ONE EDGE OF BAND, FOLD
OVER AND HEM TO
STITCH LINE.

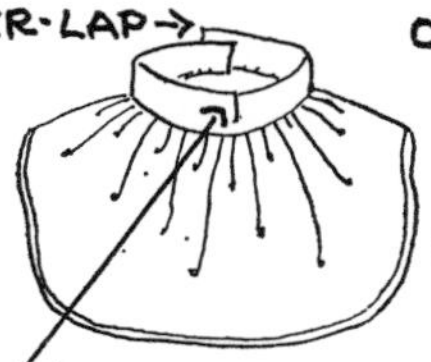

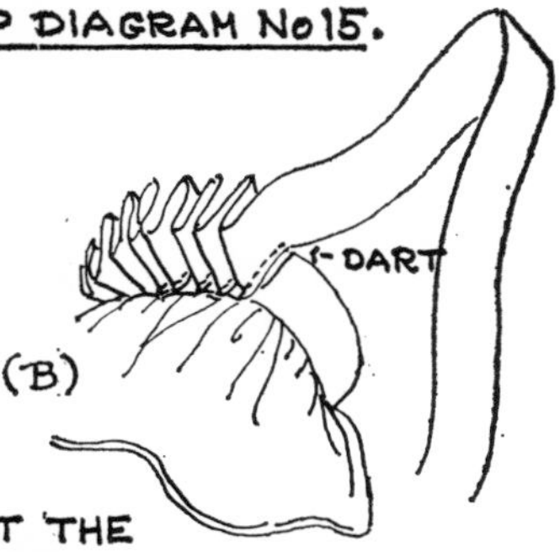

OVER-LAP →

(A)

DART

(B)

MAKE DART ½"
TO NOTHING.

BEGIN AT THE
CENTRE FRONT, SEWING THE PLASTIC
STRIP IN A ZIG-ZAG ONTO THE BAND.
THE STRIP SHOULD BE 1½" WIDE FOR 1550
RUFF, ELIZABETHAN RUFF 4" OR 5" WIDE.

STITCH UP CENTRE
BACK SEAMS, PRESS
OPEN. MACHINE
MATERIAL AND LAYERS
OF NYLON NET TO-
GETHER ROUND OUTER
EDGE. TURN RIGHT-SIDE
OUT AND PRESS. FINISH WITH TWO
OR MORE ROWS OF MACHINE STITCH.

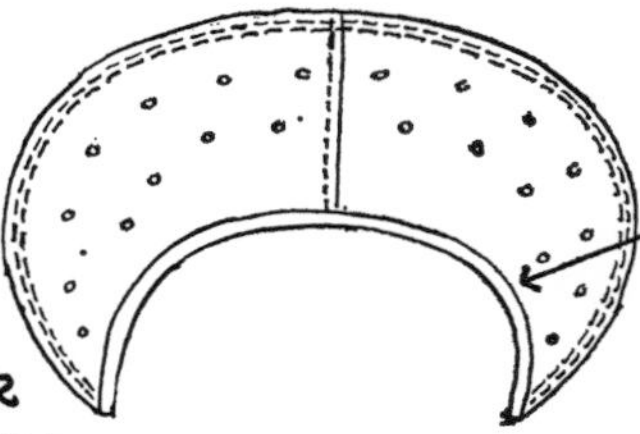

1590 COLLAR.

EDGE WITH BIAS
BINDING. PEARLS
AND SEQUINS CAN
BE ADDED FOR
ORNAMENT.

PADDED ROLL
1590.

UNSHAPED
FOAM →

(A)

POLYESTER FOAM
SHAPED WITH SHARP KNIFE
READY TO BE COVERED

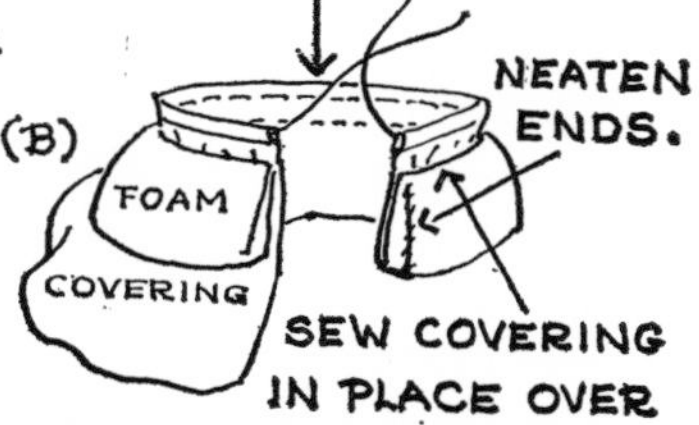

HEMMED EDGE FOR
ELASTIC OR TAPE.

(B)

FOAM
COVERING

NEATEN
ENDS.

SEW COVERING
IN PLACE OVER
POLYESTER FOAM ON THIS LINE.

Another very practical substitute for the farthingale, and in later periods for the hoop and bustle, is made of polyester foam covered with material, and tied round the waist with tapes. For the farthingale the foam is cut or curved round the hips, leaving a gap of not less than 6 inches at the centre front. It should be 2 inches deep and 3 or 4 inches wide, the width will depend on the social importance of the character, 3 inches is a good practical width and a 38 inch hip the best average size.

Shape the polyester foam with a sharp knife so that it curves off to nothing at the upper and centre front edges. Cut a piece of material (old sheeting will do) long and deep enough to cover the foam and extend 3 inches beyond its upper edge. Turn over the top of the material to make a ¾-inch hem through which a tape should be run to tie the farthingale in place. The lower edge of the material is turned up and over the foam and stitched down, the front ends are folded neatly and stitched in place (see Diagram 15, p. 45).

The padding will then rest on the hips and not make an ugly bulge at the waist itself. Basically the same method is used when hoops or a bustle is required, layouts are given for each style in the relevant chapter.

The *stomacher* is very typical of the period and was often made of the same material as the underskirt. Cut out as shown in Layout 7, p. 48, in material and thick Vilene for facing, dart separately at bust level. Sew two strips of bias binding onto the Vilene in a V shape from the bottom to the dart points. Stitch all round by machine except across the straight top, turn right side out and press (the bias must be on the outside of the Vilene). Slip-stitch the top edges together and sew 'jewels' onto the stomacher if richness is required, in any case the two layers of material should be stitched together in places with a few strong stitches. Whale bone is slipped into the bias binding, though this is usually made of plastic today; this will keep the stomacher correctly ridged (see Diagram 16, p. 49).

The underskirt is really an under apron held in place at the back by tapes. The decorative material can be sewn onto a piece of old sheet and can taper from 8 inches wide at the top to 18 inches at the bottom, thus saving on the more expensive materials. The edge of the 3 inch wide turning on the basic skirt is slip-stitched onto the under skirt in a wide V shape, the same method should be used when the under skirt was worn in the previous reign (see Layout 7, p. 48).

Sleeves were very decorative, sometimes slashed down the top from shoulder to wrist and a strip of contrasting material let in which showed in between the points where a jewel held the main sleeve together. Another version is made by using an ordinary straight sleeve pattern and cutting it down from the shoulder seam notch to the wrist, adding 1½ inches on each edge at the top and curving down to nothing just above the wrist. Sew together with either plain or contrasting piping; the extra fullness at the top may be gathered or darted to fit the armhole measurement (see Layout 7; and Diagram 14, p. 44).

The extended shoulder piece was still sometimes worn as it was in Mary Tudor's time, but now more often padded and decorated with bands of contrasting material. All these additions must work in with colour scheme and decoration of the dress as a whole. The method for making is the same as previously described, but wadding is added for the padded version.

Towards the end of her reign, Elizabeth favoured the high stand away collar of fine linen or lace. This is easily made by cutting according to Layout 8,

MARY 1. 1553-58.

ILLUSTRATION No 5.

COUNTRY WOMAN OR SERVANT.

1553 →

← 1550

ELIZABETH 1558 – 1603.

COURT DRESS 1590.

1580 →

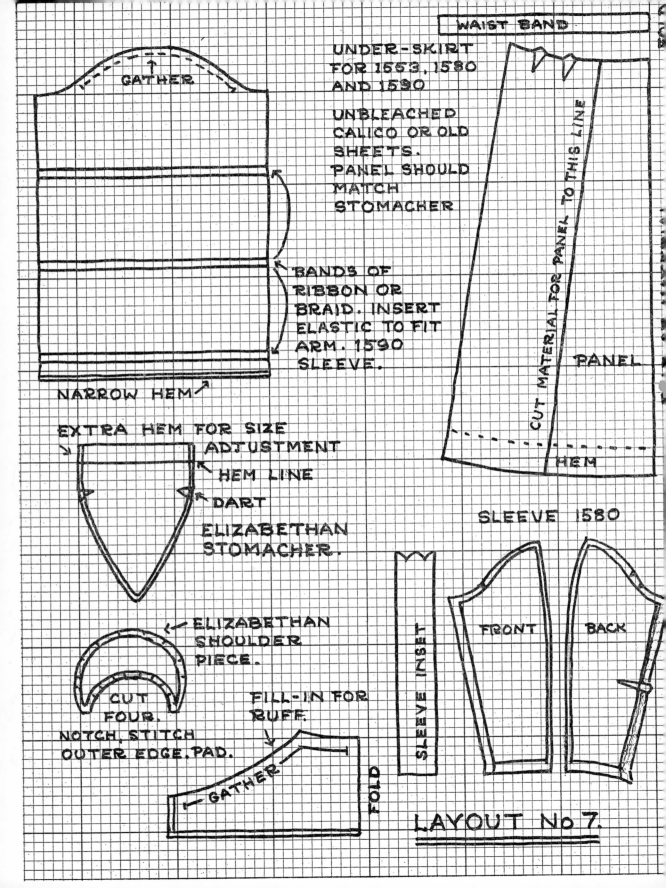

WAIST BAND

GATHER

UNDER-SKIRT FOR 1553, 1580 AND 1590

UNBLEACHED CALICO OR OLD SHEETS. PANEL SHOULD MATCH STOMACHER

CUT MATERIAL FOR PANEL TO THIS LINE

BANDS OF RIBBON OR BRAID. INSERT ELASTIC TO FIT ARM. 1590 SLEEVE.

PANEL

NARROW HEM

HEM

EXTRA HEM FOR SIZE ADJUSTMENT

HEM LINE

DART

ELIZABETHAN STOMACHER.

SLEEVE 1580

ELIZABETHAN SHOULDER PIECE.

CUT FOUR. NOTCH, STITCH OUTER EDGE. PAD.

FILL-IN FOR RUFF.

GATHER

SLEEVE INSET

FOLD

FRONT

BACK

LAYOUT No 7.

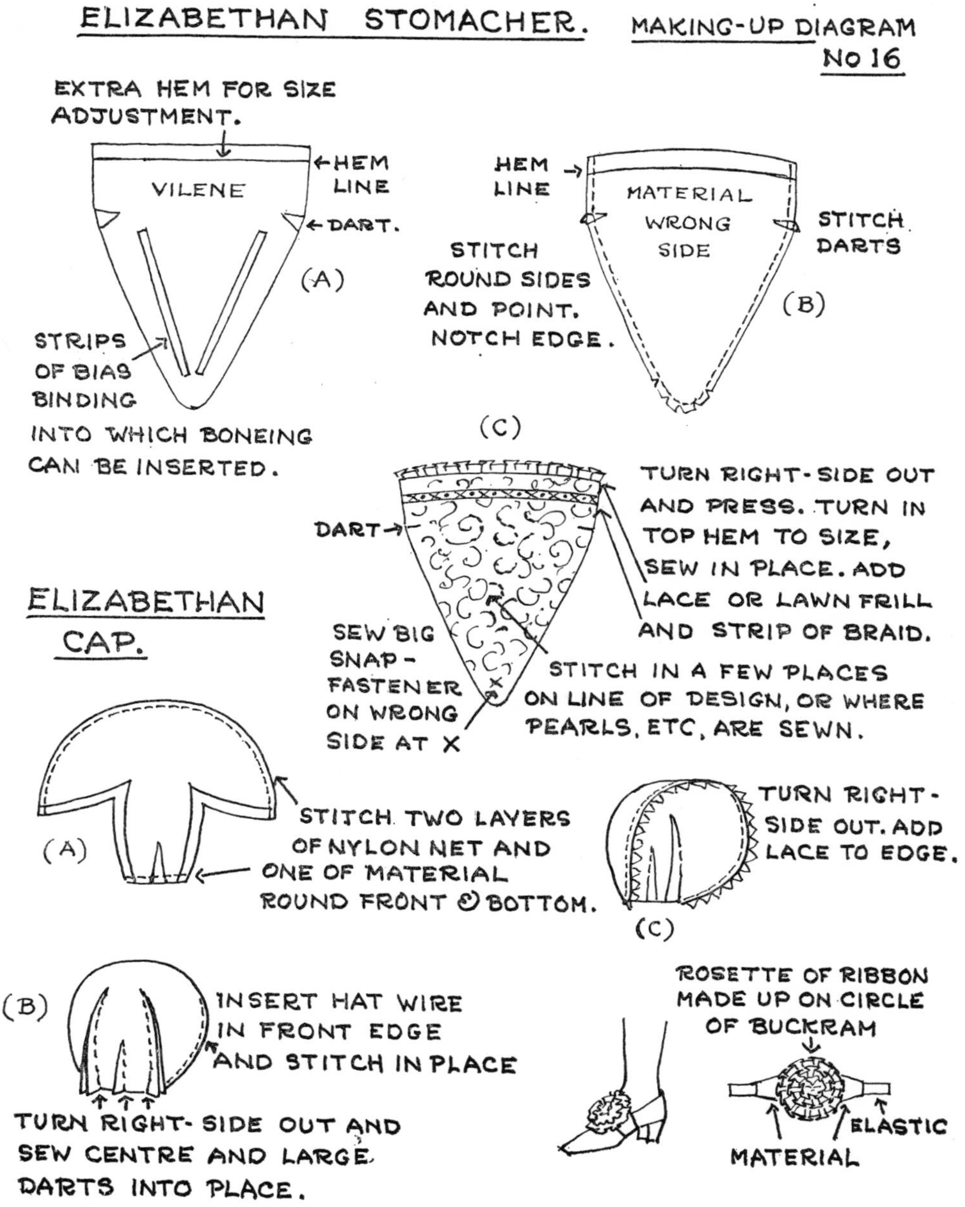

ELIZABETHAN STOMACHER.   MAKING-UP DIAGRAM
No 16

EXTRA HEM FOR SIZE
ADJUSTMENT.

←HEM
LINE

VILENE

←DART.

(A)

STRIPS
OF BIAS
BINDING
INTO WHICH BONEING
CAN BE INSERTED.

HEM →
LINE

MATERIAL
WRONG
SIDE

STITCH
DARTS

STITCH
ROUND SIDES
AND POINT.
NOTCH EDGE.

(B)

(C)

DART→

TURN RIGHT-SIDE OUT
AND PRESS. TURN IN
TOP HEM TO SIZE,
SEW IN PLACE. ADD
LACE OR LAWN FRILL
AND STRIP OF BRAID.

ELIZABETHAN
CAP.

SEW BIG
SNAP-
FASTENER
ON WRONG
SIDE AT X

STITCH IN A FEW PLACES
ON LINE OF DESIGN, OR WHERE
PEARLS, ETC, ARE SEWN.

(A)

STITCH TWO LAYERS
OF NYLON NET AND
ONE OF MATERIAL
ROUND FRONT & BOTTOM.

TURN RIGHT-
SIDE OUT. ADD
LACE TO EDGE.

(C)

(B)

INSERT HAT WIRE
IN FRONT EDGE
AND STITCH IN PLACE

TURN RIGHT-SIDE OUT AND
SEW CENTRE AND LARGE
DARTS INTO PLACE.

ROSETTE OF RIBBON
MADE UP ON CIRCLE
OF BUCKRAM

ELASTIC

MATERIAL

p. 51, thin white material or lace and one or two layers of millinery white nylon net. Sew round the outer edge, turn right side out and press, then edge with two or three rows of machine stitching; a zig-zag stitch is very effective and lace can be added if required. Finish the neck edge with inch wide white bias binding, slip-stitching half the collar to the dress and safety pinning the other half in place when the dress is on. This collar washes well and keeps its stiffness without the aid of starch or wires (see Diagram 15, p. 45).

The hood with the under cap remained in use for the first part of the reign though it was very much smaller, and more hair showed at the front. The style of dressing the hair had changed completely, it was now brushed up over a roll that went from ear to ear. In the latter part of the reign the hood had gone except for the elderly or unfashionable, and a small cap was worn covering only the back of the head. For ladies of birth and especially the Queen, this would have been made of lace, a design with a pointed edge being much favoured. Old lace doyleys are excellent for these caps and can often be found at Jumble Sales, all they will need is to be starched and two darts made at the back, with a few pearls sewn on for rich people (see Diagram 16, p. 49).

For the additions it is important to choose fabrics in a Tudor type design such as stylised intwined leaves or the five-sided rose, and this is not very difficult as in furnishing materials these designs are still used today.

Suitable colours. All the basic colours were still worn, but addition could well be made with flame, orange, gold and all the tawny shades in mind. Perhaps they were so fashionable as a compliment to Elizabeth's red hair. Poorer people would have worn plainer, duller colours, so keep these additions darker.

Jewellery. Ear-rings were now very fashionable, particularly big pearl ones, and necklaces were worn when the ruff was not, though long, gold chains were worn with all styles. Rings were also much in favour, the index and third finger being the most popular positions.

Shoes. With squared toes and in the latter part of the reign small heels, the shoes were often decorated with a large rosette. This effect can be achieved by masking an ordinary small heeled shoe with a rosette held in place *under* the instep with a 2 inch wide piece of elastic coloured to match the shoe (see Diagram 16, p. 49).

PLAYS

Elizabeth I has had as many plays written about her as ever Henry VIII's wives had written about them, and a great many are for women only; in fact the list is so long it would be invidious to mention just a few.

The Devils
Will Shakespear
Vivat, Vivat Regina
Twelfth Night
As You Like It
The Taming of the Shrew

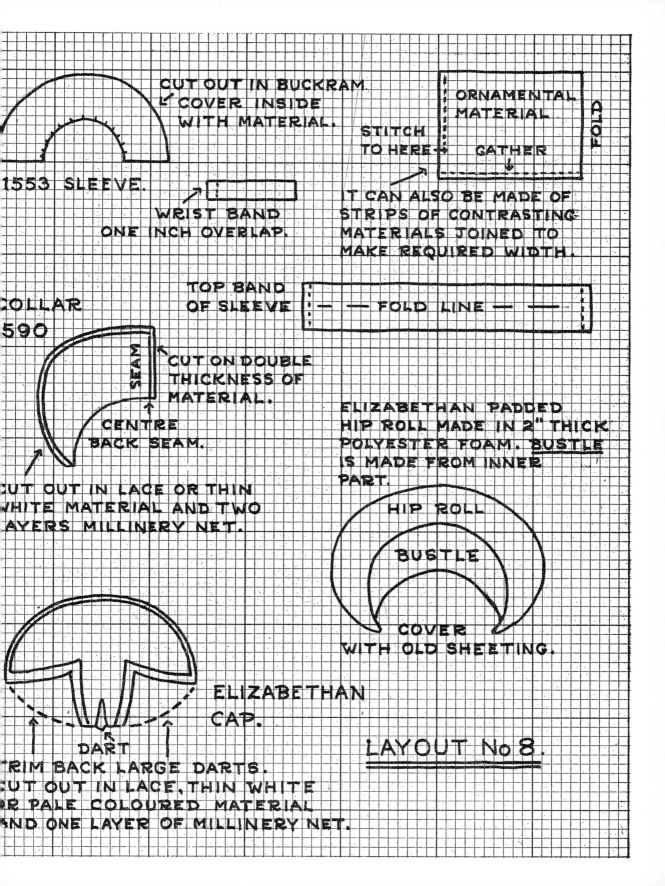

CUT OUT IN BUCKRAM.
COVER INSIDE
WITH MATERIAL.

1553 SLEEVE.

WRIST BAND
ONE INCH OVERLAP.

STITCH
TO HERE→

ORNAMENTAL
MATERIAL

GATHER

FOLD

IT CAN ALSO BE MADE OF
STRIPS OF CONTRASTING
MATERIALS JOINED TO
MAKE REQUIRED WIDTH.

COLLAR
590

TOP BAND
OF SLEEVE

— — FOLD LINE — —

SEAM

CUT ON DOUBLE
THICKNESS OF
MATERIAL.

CENTRE
BACK SEAM.

CUT OUT IN LACE OR THIN
WHITE MATERIAL AND TWO
LAYERS MILLINERY NET.

ELIZABETHAN PADDED
HIP ROLL MADE IN 2" THICK
POLYESTER FOAM. BUSTLE
IS MADE FROM INNER
PART.

HIP ROLL

BUSTLE

COVER
WITH OLD SHEETING.

DART

TRIM BACK LARGE DARTS.
CUT OUT IN LACE, THIN WHITE
OR PALE COLOURED MATERIAL
AND ONE LAYER OF MILLINERY NET.

ELIZABETHAN
CAP.

LAYOUT No 8.

Variation No. 5.   Charles I, 1625–49

There do not seem to be many plays written about this period perhaps because, except for losing his head at the end of the Civil War, Charles I does not make a good subject for drama. He was 'A loving husband and a good father' therefore there were no Mistresses or change of wives to make an emotional storm centre for a play. It is all Politics, Parliaments and Taxation, with the scaffold at the end, though he gave up his life with courage and dignity.

From the point of view of dress the reign marked a big change of style: the ruff and stomacher disappeared, so did the farthingale, the skirt now fell soft and full to the ground. The clothes for women were attractive, being less flamboyant than the men's and in better taste, in fact except for details of trimming, modern paper patterns could be adapted for these dresses. Very pointed lace was the most popular trimming, it was used round the square neck-line which was often given an off-shoulder line by a curved shaped addition with the lace extending across the edge (see Illustration 6, p. 53). The sleeves of the Royalist ladies were full, darted at the top to fit the armhole, then gathered into a band below the elbow, and ending in a lace frill or a turned back cuff with a lace edge. Another fashion note is the 'crenelated' *peplum*, this should be made of the same material as the basic dress and lined with Vilene, the 'crenelations' bound round with a contrasting colour and held in place by a narrow sash of the same material (see Illustration 6, Layout 9, p. 54 and Diagram 17, p. 55 for sleeves and peplum).

The Puritan element now coming into being divided the clothes world both for men and women, and the style of dress continued into the next reign for plays set in America, such as *The Crucible*. The women wore a plain dress for which the 'basic' dress is most suitable. The low neck should be filled in even though the very large white collars left hardly anything to 'fill in', but smaller collars were sometimes worn and give a bit of variety if a play is all Puritan (see Layout 9 and Diagram 18, p. 57). The long basic sleeve can be used or one rather fuller at the top, and either darted or gathered to fit the armhole; a plain white cap completed the attire. 'Quakers' are often mistakenly equated with Puritans, and though George Fox the founder of The Society of Friends did advise simplicity in dress he wore his hair long, not cropped like a Puritan. In fact the 'Quakers' as they were nicknamed, were more often imprisoned during the Puritan Commonwealth than in the reign of Charles II. As far as clothes are concerned the 'Quaker' grey was probably not worn till the late seventeenth and eighteenth century, and then not by all, though Elizabeth Fry became a 'plain' Quaker and wore the grey, and this was in the early nineteenth century. Bear these facts in mind when dressing a Quaker play (see Layout 10, p. 58 for plain cap).

Hair was taken back from the forehead into a bun at the crown of the head, but the side hair was left loose in curls and ringlets. Puritan women mostly wore theirs tucked in under plain white caps, but a few young and more skittish ones might have shown a curl or two.

Jewellery was fairly simple, pearls continued in favour and with the shorter sleeves, bracelets became fashionable.

Suitable Colours. Yellow and blues were very popular but brown purple-red

ILLUSTRATION No 6.

CHARLES 11
1660-85.

CHARLES 1.
1630-49.

PURITAN
1649-

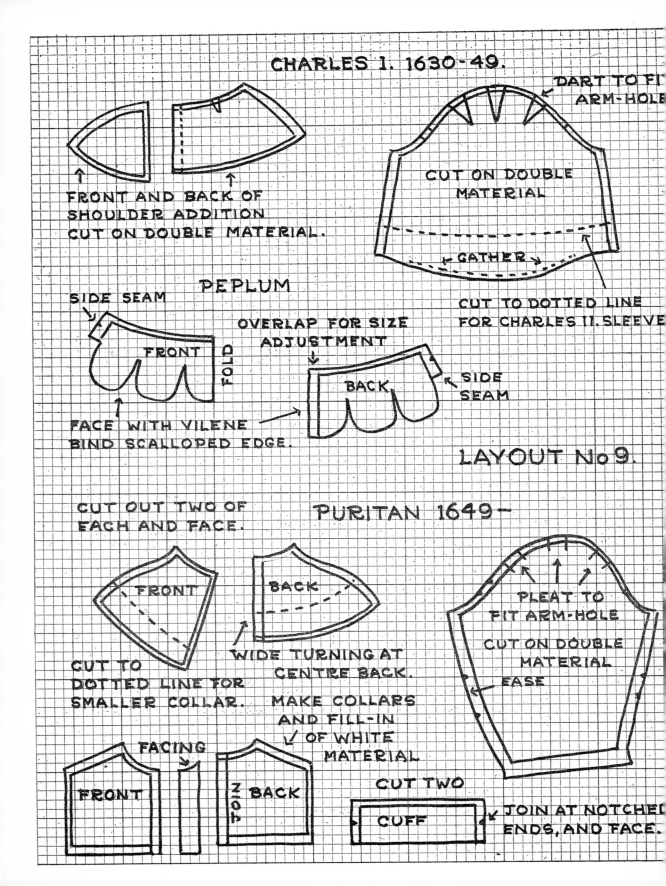

CHARLES 1. 1630-49.

FRONT AND BACK OF
SHOULDER ADDITION
CUT ON DOUBLE MATERIAL.

DART TO FIT ARM-HOLE

CUT ON DOUBLE MATERIAL

GATHER

CUT TO DOTTED LINE FOR CHARLES II. SLEEVE

PEPLUM

SIDE SEAM

FRONT

FOLD

OVERLAP FOR SIZE ADJUSTMENT

BACK

SIDE SEAM

FACE WITH VILENE BIND SCALLOPED EDGE.

LAYOUT No 9.

CUT OUT TWO OF EACH AND FACE.

PURITAN 1649~

FRONT

BACK

PLEAT TO FIT ARM-HOLE

CUT ON DOUBLE MATERIAL

EASE

CUT TO DOTTED LINE FOR SMALLER COLLAR.

WIDE TURNING AT CENTRE BACK.

MAKE COLLARS AND FILL-IN OF WHITE MATERIAL

FACING

FRONT

FOLD

BACK

CUT TWO

CUFF

JOIN AT NOTCHED ENDS, AND FACE.

CHARLES 1. 1630.

MAKING-UP DIAGRAM No 17.

"OFF-SHOULDER ADDITION"

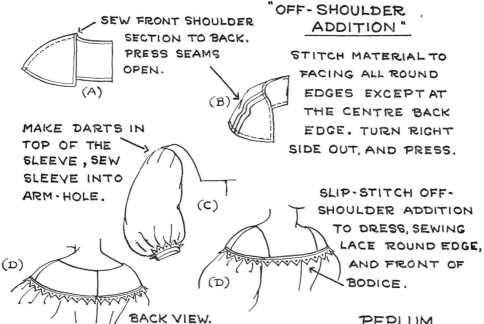

SEW FRONT SHOULDER SECTION TO BACK. PRESS SEAMS OPEN.

(A)

(B)

STITCH MATERIAL TO FACING ALL ROUND EDGES EXCEPT AT THE CENTRE BACK EDGE. TURN RIGHT SIDE OUT, AND PRESS.

MAKE DARTS IN TOP OF THE SLEEVE, SEW SLEEVE INTO ARM-HOLE.

(C)

SLIP-STITCH OFF-SHOULDER ADDITION TO DRESS, SEWING LACE ROUND EDGE, AND FRONT OF BODICE.

(D)

(D)

BACK VIEW.

PEPLUM.

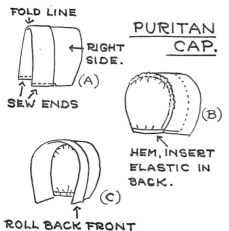

FOLD LINE

RIGHT SIDE.

(A)

SEW ENDS

PURITAN CAP.

(B)

HEM, INSERT ELASTIC IN BACK.

(C)

ROLL BACK FRONT

SEW MATERIAL AND VILENE FACING TOGETHER AT SIDE SEAMS AS IF ONE LAYER OF MATERIAL.

STITCH BOW HERE

CUT STRIPS OF MATERIAL ON BIAS, AND BIND EDGE. USE SAME MATERIAL ON STRAIGHT FOR WAIST-BAND AND BOW.

(blackberry) and greens were also worn by Royalist ladies. Grey, dove-grey and dark blue would be right for the Puritan women.

Shoes. These were square toed and high at the front, sometimes trimmed with a rosette but more often with a buckle. To make the necessary masking, cut out a piece of felt (as shown in Diagram 18, p. 57) in black or brown to match a modern squared toed shoe, and cover with black or Fablon, which will look like leather. Make a buckle by cutting out the shape in cardboard, and covering it with metal foil, stitch to the masking section with grey thread. Sew wide dark elastic to the sides to hold masking in place.

Variation No. 6. Charles II, 1660–85

This was another age of extravagance in dress, the court set the pace and the people followed as their purses permitted, and sometimes, to judge by Mr. Pepys' remarks about his own clothes, much more than they could afford. As so often happens during a period of extravagance good taste was lost in a welter of show; lace and ribbons were everywhere, and this was as much, if not more the case with men's clothes than with women's.

The neck-line was now low and boat-shaped, therefore the square neck of the basic dress should be masked by a deep frill of lace, so fashionable at this time. To hold this in place the lace is sewn to a wide strip of the same material as the dress, cut on the cross so that it will adapt to the curve. This is tacked to the neck close to the bodice line at the back and shoulder, curved past the square corner, and stitched again to the centre few inches, the width of the material filling in the corner part, and the frill of lace covering all (see Diagram 19, p. 59). The same lace should be used at the bottom of the sleeves, which were now shorter and ended above the elbow. Do not be daunted by the expense of all this lace. Cheap lace with an over-all design can be cut into bands as required, and edged with a zig-zag machine stitch, a good effect that will cost a fraction of the price of lace edging of the same width.

The sleeves were full and often slashed, the under-sleeve which showed in between the slashing should match the additions to the bodice and/or the petti-coat. This slashed sleeve is easier to make than it would seem. First cut out the full under-sleeve, using the same Layout (9, p. 54) as for the Charles I sleeve but cutting to the dotted line, then cut strips of the same material as the dress; they should be about 2 inches wide and add up to the width of the under-sleeve, turn over the edges and oversew with a zig-zag machine stitch. Tack them into place along the lower edge of the sleeve and then to the upper edge; they must lie flat but be a little longer than the under-sleeve; finally trim them to the shape of the top of the sleeve. Next machine up the seams of the under-sleeve, being careful not to catch in the 'slashings', then run a gathering thread along the top of the sleeve, using double thread, and finish by sewing lace to the bottom edge and facing it back with bias binding, through which a piece of elastic should be threaded to fit the size of the arm. The upper gathering thread is then pulled up to fit the armhole, and a 'staying' row of back-stitch put in by hand (see Diagram 20, p. 61).

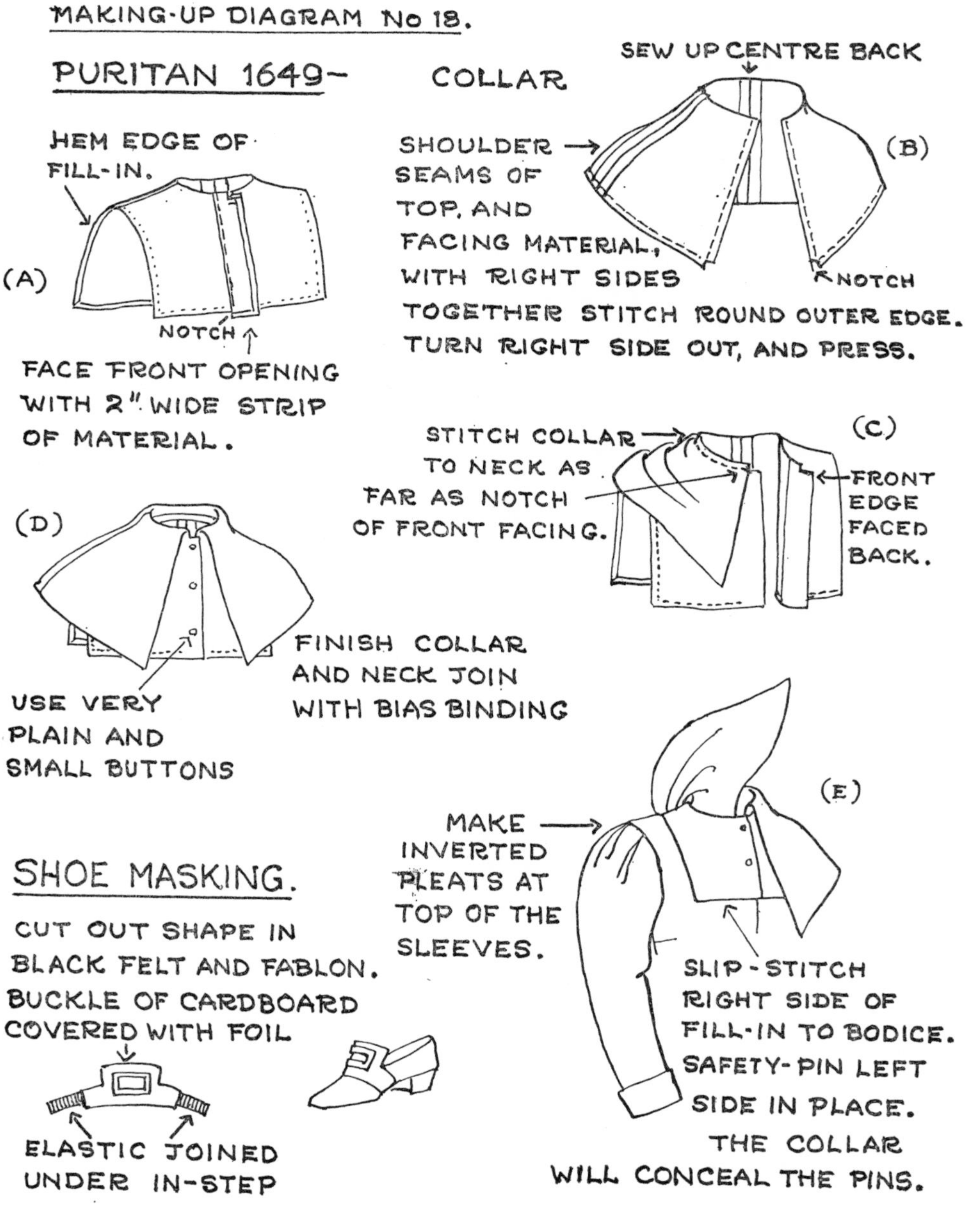

MAKING-UP DIAGRAM No 18.

PURITAN 1649—

HEM EDGE OF FILL-IN.

(A)

NOTCH ↑

FACE FRONT OPENING WITH 2" WIDE STRIP OF MATERIAL.

COLLAR

SEW UP CENTRE BACK

SHOULDER → SEAMS OF TOP, AND FACING MATERIAL, WITH RIGHT SIDES TOGETHER STITCH ROUND OUTER EDGE. TURN RIGHT SIDE OUT, AND PRESS.

(B)

NOTCH

STITCH COLLAR → TO NECK AS FAR AS NOTCH OF FRONT FACING.

(C)

FRONT EDGE FACED BACK.

(D)

USE VERY PLAIN AND SMALL BUTTONS

FINISH COLLAR AND NECK JOIN WITH BIAS BINDING

SHOE MASKING.

CUT OUT SHAPE IN BLACK FELT AND FABLON. BUCKLE OF CARDBOARD COVERED WITH FOIL

ELASTIC JOINED UNDER IN-STEP

MAKE → INVERTED PLEATS AT TOP OF THE SLEEVES.

(E)

SLIP-STITCH RIGHT SIDE OF FILL-IN TO BODICE. SAFETY-PIN LEFT SIDE IN PLACE. THE COLLAR WILL CONCEAL THE PINS.

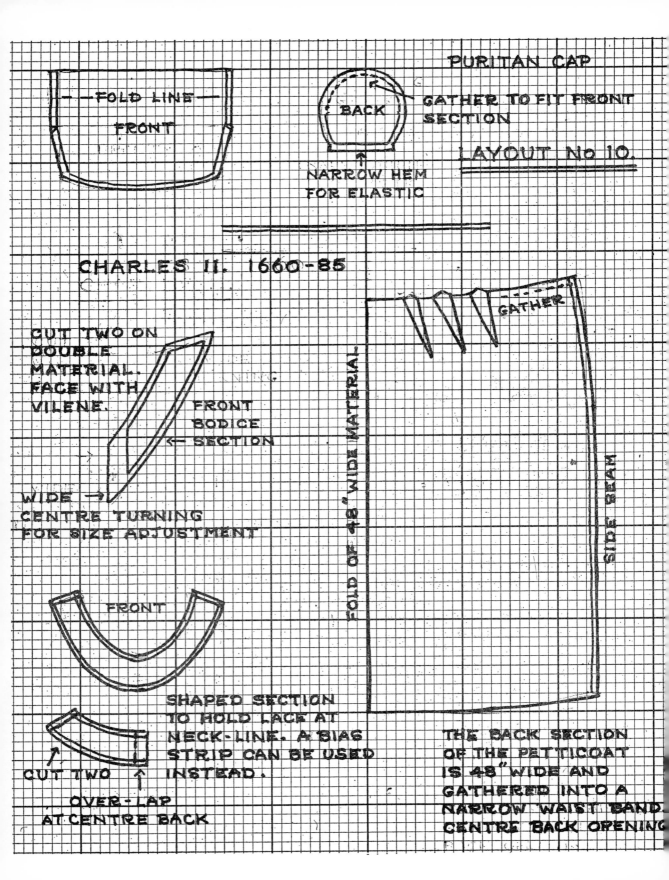

PURITAN CAP

FOLD LINE

FRONT

BACK

GATHER TO FIT FRONT SECTION

LAYOUT No 10.

NARROW HEM FOR ELASTIC

CHARLES II. 1660-85

CUT TWO ON DOUBLE MATERIAL. FACE WITH VILENE.

FRONT BODICE SECTION

GATHER

WIDE → CENTRE TURNING FOR SIZE ADJUSTMENT

FOLD OF 48" WIDE MATERIAL

SIDE SEAM

FRONT

SHAPED SECTION TO HOLD LACE AT NECK-LINE. A BIAS STRIP CAN BE USED INSTEAD.

CUT TWO

OVER-LAP AT CENTRE BACK

THE BACK SECTION OF THE PETTICOAT IS 48" WIDE AND GATHERED INTO A NARROW WAIST BAND. CENTRE BACK OPENING.

CHARLES 11. 1660-85.

MAKING-UP DIAGRAM No 19.

SEW UP SHOULDER SEAMS
OF NECK-LINE ADDITION.

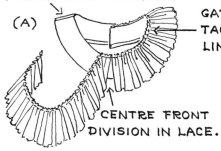

(A)

CENTRE FRONT
DIVISION IN LACE.

NECK-LINE MASKING.

TAKE TWO LENGTHS OF
LACE 7$\frac{1}{2}$" DEEP AND EACH
ONE YARD LONG. RUN A
GATHERING THREAD $\frac{1}{2}$" FROM EDGE.
TACK GATHERED LACE TO NECK-
LINE ADDITION. STITCH IN PLACE.

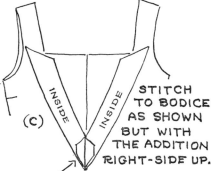

HEM →
EDGE

(B)

NOTCH NECK EDGE
TURN OVER WITH
GATHERED LACE EDGE. RUN A
LINE OF MACHINE STITCHING TO
FINISH OFF NECK-LINE.

FACE, ALSO
INTER-FACE
WITH VILENE.
SEW ALL THREE
LAYERS TOGETHER
EXCEPT AT THE
CENTRE FRONT.
TURN RIGHT-SIDE
OUT AND PRESS.

(A)

(B)

WITH RIGHT SIDES
TOGETHER, SEW
CENTRE FRONTS
TOGETHER.
ADJUST FOR
SIZE HERE.

INSIDE

(C)

INSIDE   INSIDE

STITCH
TO BODICE
AS SHOWN
BUT WITH
THE ADDITION
RIGHT-SIDE UP.

FOLD BACK UNUSED
TURNING AND STITCH
NEATLY IN PLACE.

'V' BODICE ADDITION.

The bodice, which was very fitted, had a V-shaped front that came down to a point over the skirt (see Illustration 6, p. 53, and Diagram 19, p. 59). The addition required to give this effect should be made of the same material as the petticoat, or of a piece insertion to match the lace of the frill, in either case it must be faced with heavyweight Vilene (see Layout 10, p. 58). The top edge of the V thus made is sewn from the corner of the neck-line to the arm-hole, then slip-stitched all round onto the bodice, the point of the V being held to the skirt with a large snap-fastener. The skirt either fell soft and full from the waist to the ground, and was trimmed down the front with a panel of patterned material, in which case the same material should be used for the under-sleeve, or it was caught up behind with a clasp or ribbons to show the petticoat (see Illustration 6, p. 53).

Hair. The style had changed very little, though the ringlets were now held out by false hair to give a wider line. A small fringe was fashionable and bows of ribbon were worn at the sides of the bun at the top of the ringlets. Masks came into fashion.

Jewellery. Pearls were still in favour for necklaces and bracelets and ear-rings were fashionable again.

Suitable Colours. Blues, yellows, rose red, russet browns were still popular, but the pattern on the additions should now be flowered. Many such designs are used today in furnishing fabrics, especially cotton satins and cretonnes. Elderly women often wore the Puritan type cap, servants and country people would have worn it as well.

Shoes were basically the same but had a daintier heel, and for rich people the masking could be covered with brocade.

PLAYS

As, unlike his father, Charles II had plenty of mistresses many plays have been written about him and them. It is also the period of Restoration Comedies, but there is often confusion about dressing these. For instance *The Way of the World* by Congreve, and *The Beaux' Stratagem* by Farquhar were produced in 1700 and 1707 respectively, and so should be dressed in the William and Mary, early Queen Anne costume. Vanbrugh was born and lived in the Restoration Period, but his most famous play *The Relapse* was not produced till 1696. Dryden, Wycherley, and Molière were unquestionably of the Restoration, i.e. Charles II period; here are some plays of that time.

The Country Wife
A Woman Killed with Kindness
Sir Martin Mar-all
The Imaginary Invalid
The Prodigeous Snob
The School for Wives
And so to Bed, a modern play about Mr. Pepys

CHARLES 11. 1660-85.

MAKING-UP DIAGRAM No 20.

SLASHED SLEEVE.

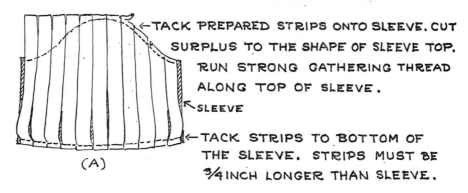

←TACK PREPARED STRIPS ONTO SLEEVE. CUT SURPLUS TO THE SHAPE OF SLEEVE TOP. RUN STRONG GATHERING THREAD ALONG TOP OF SLEEVE.

↖SLEEVE

←TACK STRIPS TO BOTTOM OF THE SLEEVE. STRIPS MUST BE ¾ INCH LONGER THAN SLEEVE.

(A)

(B)

STITCH LACE AND 2" WIDE BIAS STRIP OF MATERIAL TO BOTTOM OF SLEEVE. TURN OVER BIAS AND STITCH TO SLEEVE BY HAND. INSERT ELASTIC TO FIT ARM.

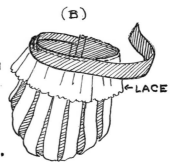

←LACE

PULL UP TOP GATHERING THREAD TO FIT ARM-HOLE.

SHOE MASKING.

PEARLS SEWN IN SHAPE OF A BUCKLE

ELASTIC JOINED UNDER INSTEP.

FELT-BACKED FABLON STUCK TO A TOP OF PLAIN MATERIAL OR BROCADE. PAINT SHOE TO TONE.

Variation No. 7.   William and Mary, 1689–1702

In this joint reign the influence of the court on clothes began to wane, and prominent men and women influenced fashion to a greater extent. What ever the origin there was a big change of style at this time.

The skirt of the dress was now looped up at the back over the petticoat or under-skirt in a way that resembles the bustle of Victorian times (see Layout 8, p. 51), though the high fronted head-dress of lace and ribbons has so far remained peculiar to this period. A broad band of material edged the neck-line which was now a soft V, and continued down the front of the bodice meeting edge to edge, and often held together with buttons or loops of braid. It was usually made of material that contrasted with the main dress, and was either patterned, or a plain dark colour; the cuff on the sleeve would be faced with the same material. Sometimes the bodice band appeared to continue onto the skirt, in which case the 3 inch turning on the centre front seam should be faced back to match the bodice. To make this bodice addition follow Layout 11, p. 64, cutting heavyweight Vilene to the same shape. Join the material and Vilene separately at the shoulder seams, press them open and, placing right sides together, machine leaving the ends open, pull through and press. Match the front edges and stitch together at the point where the bottoms or braid loops will be sewn. Slip-stitch the addition to the basic bodice, taking care to sew it very firmly at the square corner of the neck. Add a frill of thin white material to the inside of the neck-line. Terylene and cotton mixtures are the best as they do not crease easily; the same material should be used for the white under-sleeves. To achieve variety knots of ribbon can be sewn to the shoulders of some dresses (see Illustration 7, p. 71 and Diagram 21, p. 65).

The petticoat, or more exactly under-skirt, was frequently decorated with rows of embroidery which can be simulated by using material which has a dainty floral design in stripes. Wide nylon curtain net could also be used but must of course be gathered onto a lining; an old piece of sheet in white, or dyed a pale colour, would be cheap and perfectly adequate. A bustle must be made to support the back of the skirt, and give the necessary jutting out line. For this buy 2 inch thick polyester foam; it can be cut to shape with a sharp knife, then covered with any odd piece of material and tied on round the waist with tapes, or safety pinned to the under-skirt as it will not show. The same bustle can be used again in the Victorian period (see Layout 8, p. 51).

The sleeve was short, ending above the elbow. The basic below-elbow sleeve can be used by letting it out a little and turning up the hem; add the stand away cuff that was so much a feature of dresses at this time. Another version had a gathered top, or the fullness was taken up in an inverted pleat at the point where the shoulder seam meets the sleeve. The cuff was added to all versions. An under-sleeve of white material, which was puffed, and had one or two rows of frills or lace ended below the elbow. To make this take a piece of material 24 inches wide and 18 inches deep, seam together the 18 inch sides with a flat seam. Fold back the material onto itself at 10 inches and machine ½ inch in from the fold, through this elastic will later be threaded. Turn up a small hem on the remaining 8 inches and stitch to the 10 in depth in two rows ½ inch apart 5 inches from the bottom edge, this will also have elastic run through it to fit the arm. Before doing so a frill of lace or another frill of material can be added (see Diagram 22, p. 67 also Layout 11, p. 64 for cuff and alternative sleeve). It is always best to make under-sleeves, collars etc, as separate entities as these parts of a costume catch the make-up and therefore need to be washed or cleaned most frequently.

Hair was swept up from the face and the back hair concealed under the cap-like part of the head-dress. The front erection was usually made of lace, pleated and wired into position. With the aid of white millinery nylon net this head-dress can be made without wire (which is not only difficult to deal with, but often fails to keep the front erect) especially if nodding, head shaking or deep curtsies are part of the action in the play. Sew bands of lace about 6 or 7 inches wide to the same width of nylon net, curving off to nothing at each end. Cut a circle of thin white material large enough to cover the head from the front to the nape of the neck. Pleat the nylon backed lace onto the front half of the circle, and face back the entire circle with white bias binding. Thread narrow elastic through to fit the size of the head. Add loops of ribbon and streamers of lace at the point where the arch of lace and nylon net ends over the ears. Catch-stitch the front erection to the cap part in one or two places for extra security (see Layout 11, p. 64 and Diagram 22, p. 67).

Jewellery. Very much as before. Patches were worn on the face after 1700.

Suitable colours. Yellows, blues, apricot, browns and rose red; for additions flowered striped materials and plain contrasting colours.

Shoes were practically unchanged and, as the skirts touched the ground and sometimes even trailed on the ground at the back, they were not in evidence.

PLAYS

This might be called late 'Restoration' Comedy period.
The Relapse
The Way of the World
The Beaux' Stratagem
Viceroy Sarah
Many plays for women only about Queen Anne and Sarah Churchill.

Variation No. 8. Queen Anne and George I, 1702–27

The dress with the bustle and the high fronted head-dress were worn till 1711, and as Queen Anne died in 1714 her reign had little fashion significance. Plays about her nearly always include the 1st Duchess of Marlborough (Sarah Churchill) and, as she was practically forced to leave the court in 1711, the dresses for these plays will be of the William and Mary, early Queen Anne styles. After 1711 a change of line occurred, the bustle disappeared and the skirt spread sideways instead; this effect is achieved with stiff petticoats and/or hip pads.

To make the *hip pads* follow the same method as was used for making the bustle, but make two shapes tying them, one over each hip, with tapes (see Layout 12, p. 68 and Diagram 24, p. 72). Petticoats are a very useful part of a Drama Wardrobe as they can be used in several different periods, so good,

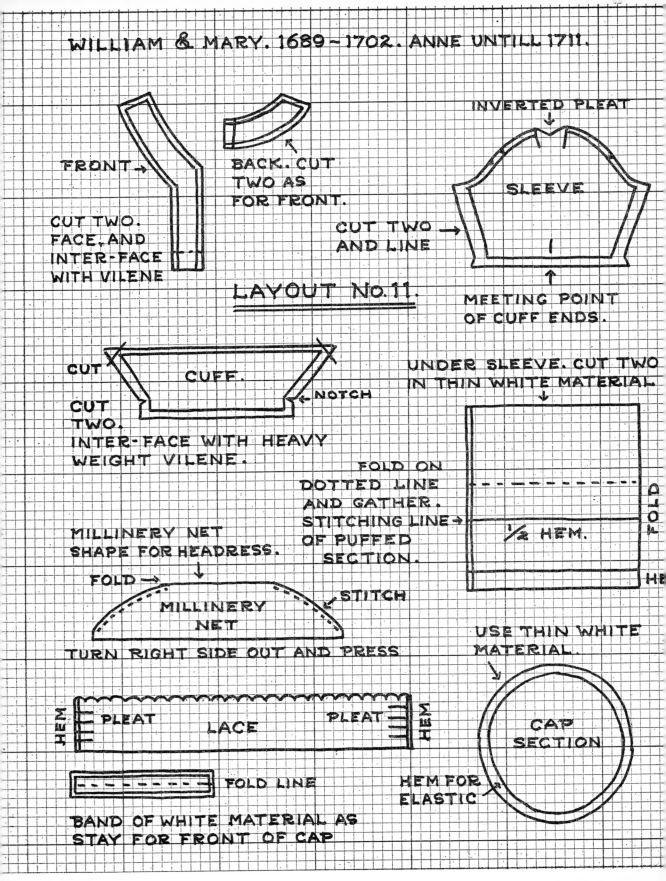

WILLIAM & MARY. 1689~1702. ANNE UNTILL 1711.

FRONT→

BACK. CUT TWO AS FOR FRONT.

CUT TWO. FACE, AND INTER-FACE WITH VILENE

INVERTED PLEAT

SLEEVE

CUT TWO → AND LINE

MEETING POINT OF CUFF ENDS.

LAYOUT No. 11.

CUT

CUFF.

CUT TWO. INTER-FACE WITH HEAVY WEIGHT VILENE.

NOTCH

UNDER SLEEVE. CUT TWO IN THIN WHITE MATERIAL

FOLD ON DOTTED LINE AND GATHER. STITCHING LINE→ OF PUFFED SECTION.

FOLD

½ HEM.

HE

MILLINERY NET SHAPE FOR HEADRESS.

FOLD →

MILLINERY NET

STITCH

TURN RIGHT SIDE OUT AND PRESS

USE THIN WHITE MATERIAL.

CAP SECTION

HEM

PLEAT

LACE

PLEAT

HEM

FOLD LINE

HEM FOR ELASTIC

BAND OF WHITE MATERIAL AS STAY FOR FRONT OF CAP

WILLAM & MARY 1689-1702. & ANNE TILL 1711.

BODICE ADDITION.

SEW UP THE
SHOULDER
SEAMS OF THE
TOP MATERIAL.
PRESS OPEN
THE SEAMS.

MAKING-UP DIAGRAM No 21.

SEW THE SEAMS
OF FACING AND
INTER-FACING TO-
GETHER AS IF THEY
WERE ONE LAYER OF
MATERIAL. TRIM BACK
INTER-FACING TO
STITCHING LINE.

←NOTCH

STITCH ROUND
EDGE, EXCEPT
THE BOTTOM.
PULL THROUGH
BOTTOM, AND
PRESS.

JOIN THE
FRONTS EDGE
TO EDGE WITH
A FEW STRONG
STITCHES, CONCEAL
WITH BUTTONS. ADD
FRILL OF PLAIN
MATERIAL AT NECK.

BOWS
OF RIBBON
WERE OFTEN
WORN ON THE
SHOULDERS

←TURN
UNDER TO
FIT LENGTH OF BODICE.

PLEAT →

SEW ROUND EDGE OF CUFF
THROUGH MATERIAL, FACING
AND INTER-FACING. TURN
RIGHT-SIDE OUT. PRESS.

CATCH-
STITCH
CUFF
HERE.

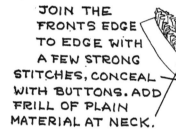

ADD BINDING TO EDGE

STITCH CUFF TO
BOTTOM OF SLEEVE.
TURN UNDER AND HEM
BACK THE BINDING.

F

practical design and care in making are very worth while (see Diagram 23, p. 69). First make a yoke by using the top 8 inches of any straight skirt pattern. Make it 4 inches larger than the minimum size and box-pleat at the side seam, including the narrow waist belt, it is thus very easy to let out; there should also be a fold over at the centre back opening. Onto the bottom of the yoke gather two widths of 48 inch wide material, or if old sheets are used, as they well could be, just join up pieces till you have the required width. As the under petticoat does not show, the number of joins will not matter. Should the sheeting be rather soft it must be starched with permanent starch. If more fullness is needed, especially at the bottom of a skirt, add a deep frill of crêpe paper, sewing it into place with a very long machine stitch. Make sure that the paper does not extend below the material as it may then get torn, though should this happen it is very easy to replace a section of the frill. More than one row of paper frills can be added according to the needs of the period.

The other big change was the *Saque*, a fashion from France. This was a loose, long over-dress falling wide and full from pleats at the back, but showing most of the dress in the front where it was held in at the waist. The Saque was usually made of contrasting material to the dress, being either patterned or of a different colour or shade. The long revers and back yoke should be of patterned material if the main section is plain, or a deeper shade of the dress if the Saque is patterned. The sleeves of the Saque are the same as the basic below elbow version, to which should be added a flared section of the same material; one or two frills of lace should be sewn to the end of the sleeve and show beyond the flared part. Silver lace was very fashionable at this time and can be made inexpensively by painting ordinary lace (which may have been found at a Jumble Sale) with silver paint. As it requires a lot of material to make the Saque old curtains should be sought, either plain or flowered; this will have a lot of money.

To make the Saque cut out as shown in Layout 12, p. 68, the deep shaped dart under the arm is the point at which adjustment of size can be made. Stitch the wide back section to the front/side section, then stitch to the yoke in one or two deep pleats (see Diagram 23 A-D, p. 69). Join the front facing to the yoke facing at the shoulder seams, then sew to the front and the under yoke, turn the facing over onto the wrong side, press, turn in a narrow hem and slip-stitch into place down the front and round the yoke (see Diagram 23E). Set in the sleeves as for an ordinary dress, then sew a large hook onto the edge of the front facing to correspond to a bar eye at the waist on the dress, so holding the Saque in position showing the front of the dress (see Diagram 23, p. 69).

The *Hair* was brushed up all round into curls at the top of the head, one or two of the curls being allowed to fall to the shoulders at the back. Wreaths of flowers and ribbons were frequently worn.

Though the folding type of fan that we know first came into use at the end of the Elizabethan period, it is most typical of the eighteenth century when no ladies' costume was complete without one, and a whole sign language of the fan developed.

Jewellery. Very little was worn, flowers and ribbons were the chief ornaments, with a small black patch high on one cheek and near the corner of the mouth on the other side.

Suitable colours. Blues, yellows, greens, greys. When flowered material is used for an addition, look for a rather more stylised design than before.

WILLIAM & MARY 1689-1702. ANNE TILL 1711.

MAKING-UP DIAGRAM No 22.

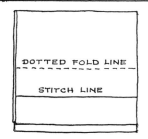

DOTTED FOLD LINE

STITCH LINE

SEW UP SIDE SEAM AND
TURN UP 1"INCH HEM AT
BOTTOM OF MATERIAL.

UNDER-SLEEVE.

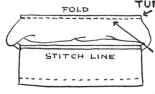

FOLD

STITCH LINE

TURN OVER ON FOLD-
LINE. STITCH
MAKING ½ INCH
HEM FOR ELASTIC.
GATHER ON FOLD-
LINE TO FIT
SLEEVE. HEM
BOTTOM EDGE.

INSERT
ELASTIC IN →
HEM TO FIT
ARM.

SEW GATHERED EDGE
TO INSIDE OF SLEEVE
ON CUFF BINDING.

HEADRESS.

NYLON NET.

LACE

PLEAT ENDS OF
LACE. GATHER
AND SEW TO NYLON
NET SHAPE.

CATCH-STITCH LACE
ONTO NET SHAPE.

PLEAT NYLON NET
AND LACE ONTO
BAND. TURN OVER
EDGE, AND HEM.

BUSTLE.

COVER POLYESTER
FOAM. SEW
LOOPS AT ENDS
FOR TAPES TO
HOLD BUSTLE IN PLACE.(SEE
ELIZABETHAN HIP-ROLL LAY-OUT
AND METHOD OF SHAPING FOAM.

←RUN ELASTIC
THROUGH CAP
←HEM. SEW TOP
PART TO BAND
ON FRONT.*
CAP HOLDS IN
HAIR. BOWS AND
STREAMERS OF LACE
CAN BE ADDED TO
THE FRONT ENDS.*

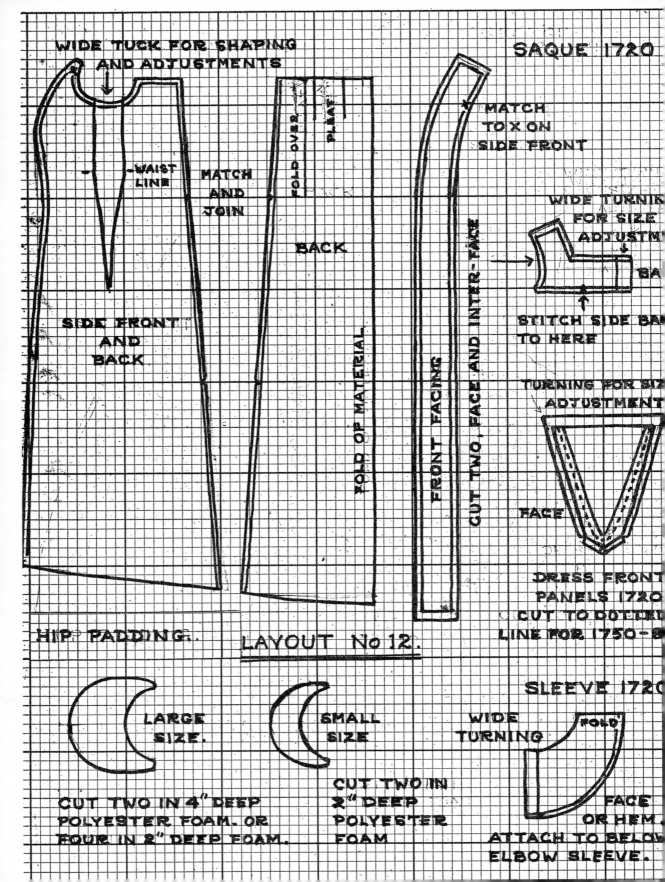

WIDE TUCK FOR SHAPING
AND ADJUSTMENTS

SAQUE 1720

WAIST LINE

MATCH AND JOIN

FOLD OVER

PLEAT

BACK

MATCH TO X ON SIDE FRONT

WIDE TURNING FOR SIZE ADJUSTM'

BA

SIDE FRONT AND BACK

STITCH SIDE BA TO HERE

TURNING FOR SIZ ADJUSTMENT

FOLD OF MATERIAL

FRONT FACING

CUT TWO, FACE AND INTER-FACE

FACE

DRESS FRONT PANELS 1720

HIP PADDING.

LAYOUT No 12.

CUT TO DOTT LINE FOR 1750-8

SLEEVE 1720

LARGE SIZE.

SMALL SIZE

WIDE TURNING

FOLD

CUT TWO IN 4" DEEP POLYESTER FOAM. OR FOUR IN 2" DEEP FOAM.

CUT TWO IN 2" DEEP POLYESTER FOAM

FACE OR HEM

ATTACH TO BELOW ELBOW SLEEVE.

QUEEN ANNE FROM 1711. GEORGE 1. 1714-27.

MAKING-UP DIAGRAM No 23.

THE SAQUE.

(A)

STITCH UP DART.

STITCH SIDE-BACK TO BACK

(C)

SEW TOP FRONT FACING TO SIDE FRONT MATCHING CROSSES

(B)

SEW UP SHOULDER SEAMS OF FRONT FACING AND BACK YOKE. ALSO YOKE CENTRE BACK. SEW UP SEAMS OF FACING. PRESS OPEN SEAMS.

(D) STITCH BACK SECTIONS. TO YOKE, SEWING PLEATS INTO PLACE.

PETTICOAT.

INVERTED PLEATS AT SIDES.

OVER-LAP AT CENTRE BACK.

(E) STITCH FACINGS TO RIGHT SIDE OF FRONTS AND YOKE. TURN OVER AND PRESS

SEW BIAS BINDING TO ARM-HOLE.

SLIP-STITCH SHOULDER AREA TOGETHER.

(F)

STITCH BACK FACINGS.

Shoes were court shaped with a more pointed toe and nearly always trimmed with a buckle.

PLAYS

Apart from ones about Queen Anne and Sarah Churchill, the Jacobite rising in Scotland is the most frequent source of dramas. This rising occurred in 1715; do not confuse this with the 1745 rising. The first was around the Old Pretender, the second involved Bonnie Prince Charlie. If a play is being produced about the 1715 Rising do bear in mind the kilt was not then worn as it is today, nor was it in such bright colours. And above all do not dress a woman in a kilt, only a man should wear one. The early "kilt" was a length of material roughly pleated into a belt; the remainder was thrown over the shoulder. See early pictures.

Variation No. 9   George II, 1727–60

Fashion was now set by the great ladies at court, very often mistresses of the French Kings, though there were other notable leaders of fashion, both men and women. Diamonds came from South America after the middle of this century, but the real brilliance of the stone was not displayed until it was faceted and the art of lapidary had been very little developed before 1746, after which time 'diamonds' may correctly glitter in the costumes of the rich, men and women alike. From the viewpoint of costume for the stage, Oliver Goldsmith was perhaps the best known English dramatist born in this reign, although he lived well into the next one, and indeed his most famous play *She Stoops to Conquer* was not produced till 1773. But when dressing this play it might be taken into account that the countrified occupants of Mr. Hardcastle's household would have worn the simpler, rather than the extreme fashions of the day, which did not vary much from 1750 to 1770. Even Mrs. Hardcastle, despite all her endeavours, may not have been *au fait* with the latest fashions, and Miss Hardcastle certainly dressed in a very simple way, as the play indicates.

The fitted bodice and small waist were unchanged, but sometimes a V-shaped section of contrasting colour was added to the front of the bodice. Though this addition is stitched to the outside, it is made to look as if it is part of an under bodice by edging it with braid or ruching to match the dress (see Diagram 25, p. 73). The skirt fell full to the ground, and was held out by stiff petticoats; sometimes it was opened down the centre front to show a contrasting under-skirt, often of flowered material.

The neck-line was square and either edged with a frill or veiled with a simple 'kerchief' type *fichu*, which was often tied in the front with a bow of ribbon. This fichu is very simple to make with 1¼ yards of plain white nylon curtain net, cut to a width of 24 inches, any that is left over will make the frill at the bottom of the sleeves. Fold lengthwise so that one layer lies an inch short of the other, curve off the ends to nothing at the fold line. Gather on the fold line for 3 or 4 inches at the back, and bind with bias binding, this will make the fichu drape well, and the binding will make it easy to safety pin it to the dress. A few horizontal tucks should be made at the back to prevent the fichu from flopping in an

ILLUSTRATION No 7.

1780

1790

1750-60

1689

1720

1689-1711.

1760-80

GEORGE 11. 1727-60.

MAKIING-UP DIAGRAM No 24.

FICHU.

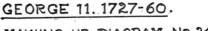

FOLD "LAWN" AND GATHER SLIGTHLY INTO BIAS BINDING.

BOW OF RIBBON TIES FRONT OF FICHU.

SEW STAYING TUCKS IN BACK.

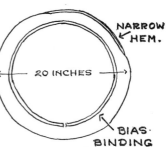

NARROW HEM.

20 INCHES

BIAS BINDING SEWN 2" INCHES FROM EDGE. RUN ELASTIC THROUGH TO FIT HEAD SIZE.

MOB CAP.

STRAW HAT.

CUT OFF TOP PART OF CROWN.

LEAVE ½ "OF CROWN ON BRIM — PETERSHAM.

RIBBON OR BIAS BINDING

CROWN STITCHED ONTO PETERSHAM.

TURN OVER AND HEM BINDING OR RIBBON.

RIBBON TIES.

SMALL HIP PADDING.

COVER POLYESTER FOAM. HOLD TOGETHER AT BACK WITH ELASTIC

LOOPS FOR TAPE OR SAFETY-PINS TO HOLD PADDING IN PLACE.

TRIM HAT WITH FLOWERS OR RUCHED RIBBON.

GEORGE III. PERIOD 1760-95.

MAKING-UP DIAGRAM No 25.

WIDE HIP PADDING.

COVER-WIDER PADDING OF
POLYESTER FOAM, THEN
STITCH TO BOTTOM EDGE
OF SMALL HIP PADDING. ADD
EXTRA STRIP OF ELASTIC.

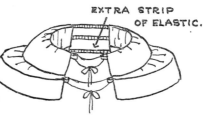

EXTRA STRIP
OF ELASTIC.

RUCHED EDGE.

WRONG SIDE.

RUCHING SEWN
TO BIAS BINDING
FOR 1760-80
NECK-LINE.
ONLY ONE SIDE
SHOWN.

LACE EDGING

1760-80 BODICE FRONT.

"LACING" AND
PART OF RUCHED
EDGING.

APRON 1790-5.

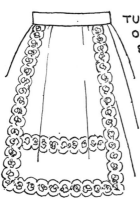

TURN OVER TOP
OF APRON AND
SLIP-STITCH TO
BOTTOM OF SKIRT
WAIST BAND.

MOB CAP. 1780 —

USE SAME
METHOD AS FOR
1750-60 CAP, BUT
CUT A CIRCLE 28"
ACROSS, OR MORE
FOR VERY HIGH CAP.
LINE INNER SIDE OF CIRCLE
WITH PALE GREY TAFFETA. MAKE
HORIZONTAL TUCKS TO GIVE
CENTRE FRONT AN UPWARD CURVE.
TRIM WITH A BOW.

unbecoming way (see Diagram 24, p. 72). Where the net requires edge-stitching a very fine thread, needle, and stitch must be used. It is of course made as a separate article so that it can be used on different dresses, and can also be washed easily.

The sleeves ended just above the elbow, sometimes they were trimmed with a row of ruching to match any used on the dress, but always ended with one or two layers of frills which sloped downwards behind the arm, and were either of lace or fine 'linen'. Very dainty aprons were worn by ladies and were varied in length. Working people and servants wore a serviceable version in stout linen.

Mob caps, at first small in size and frilled at the edge, were worn indoors and also outdoors under the pretty straw hats with shallow crowns that were fashionable then, they were tied under the chin with ribbons that held down the edge of the brim, and were often trimmed with a wreath of flowers. Working people usually wore a 'kerchief over their heads, tied under the chin just as our head scarves are today, except that they would most probably have been of plain white linen (see Diagram 24, p. 72).

Hats (see Diagram 24). Always look for old straw ones at Jumble Sales as the shape can usually be altered. The hat fashionable at this time (1750–60) had a medium size brim the same width all round, the crown was very shallow and flat on top. To alter a modern hat cut off the crown $\frac{1}{2}$ inch up from the brim, and sew by hand, using a long back stitch, onto a band of straw coloured Petersham ribbon $1\frac{1}{2}$ inches wide. Using a saucepan which measures 20 to 21 inches round, turn it upside down and pad with paper till it is slightly oval and measures about 22 inches. Buy from a chemist 1 oz of gum arabic and dissolve this in a pint of hot water. This will take some time to dissolve so prepare well beforehand, or buy a ready made straw stiffener. Whichever is used thoroughly damp the straw crown with the mixture, and press it down over the padded saucepan, moulding it to a flat topped shape with the hands; it may help to put something heavy on the top while it is left to dry. When it is dry and set in shape cut off the crown 2 inches below the flat top, marking the line with a felt pen to be sure it is even, then stitch onto the Petersham so that the two edges of the crown meet. If the brim of the modern hat is too wide, mark with a felt pen to the required size, and sew onto this line a length of matching ribbon or binding, this is best done by hand. Cut off the surplus brim and turn over the bias binding or ribbon and sew in place by machine. This is not difficult if a long stitch is used and the hat supported with the left hand. Sew ribbons to the crown where it meets the brim, at points just above the ears, they then come down over the edge of the brim, where they should be caught with a few stitches, and tie under the chin in a pretty bow. It is a very becoming fashion and a very slightly different version was worn in the Regency period. Finish with a wreath of flowers or band of ribbon either of which will cover the join in the crown.

Hair was still swept up from the face and neck to the top of the head, but less loosely than before. The curls were more formally arranged and adorned with bow of ribbon, often of black velvet as this made a good contrast to the powdered hair much favoured by fashionable ladies. When they were living at their country house they might go unpowdered, and ordinary folk certainly did.

Jewellery. Pearls were still worn tied with a bow of ribbon to form a choker necklace, and diamonds were very fashionable in the latter part of the reign, but only for rich people. Neck bands of velvet or ruched ribbon, with a flower or a small brooch as an ornament were also popular.

Suitable colours. Rose, red and yellows (with green trimmings), greys, blues or greens (trimmed with pinks). Dainty flowered patterns for aprons and under-skirts, also for the V-shaped bodice addition.

Shoes had curved 'Louis' heels and pointed toes. If it is necessary to mask a shoe or slipper use the same method as described at the end of the chapter on the Basic Gown, but use a light coloured Fablon or Brocade for the top layer, and paint the rest of the shoe with special shoe colourant.

PLAYS

During this period the second Jacobite Rising occurred in 1745, and there are many plays about Bonnie Prince Charlie and Flora Macdonald. The tartans were now more developed and precise, though the colours were still not as bright as they are today. Comment about the kilt still applies.

The Beggars Opera, 1728

Variation No. 10   George III Period, 1760–95. Lived till 1820

Though George III lived till 1820, after 1795 the French Revolution had so marked an effect on clothes that it changed the whole fashion scene, and we have the period of Greek inspired dress referred to in Chapter I. This was gradually translated into the high-waisted 'Empire' line of the Napoleonic era (Empire 1804) and then became in England the style we call Regency (1811).

It so happens that the most famous English plays, such as Sheridan's *The School for Scandal,* were written from 1775 onwards, and in the many dramas about the French Revolution it is usually the plight of the aristocrats that holds the stage, and naturally they did not wear revolutionary fashions. If any Revolutionaries do appear they are likely to be dressed in tattered old clothes, and wear a red stocking-like cap on their heads. The Greek inspired dress did not appear till after the first fury and fighting were over.

Up until 1779 the neck of the dress remained as before, square with a ruched edging, with crossed lacing doing up the front of the dress over an inset, that was of the same material as the elaborate under-skirt or 'petticoat' (see Diagram 25, p. 73). The skirt became very wide over the hips, and ladies of high fashion had to enter doors side-ways, so exaggerated did this fashion become. It is not necessary to go to such extremes, but extra padding will be needed, as well as the under petticoats described in Variation No. 8. The padding will be made by the method described there, using either thicker and wider polyester foam, or two layers held together and covered in one. When making this deeper padding cut the foam to allow for the curved shape of the hip, it must 'sit' comfortably on the body (see Diagram 25).

After 1780 clothes became simpler, the bodice was fitted as before but the crossed lacing and the square neck were replaced by a large fichu, usually with a frilled edge. This is made in the same way as the smaller one described in

Variation No. 9, but using a slightly wider nylon curtain net with a frilled edge. This type of fichu was tucked across itself into the neck of the dress (see Illustration 7, p. 71). The sleeves were still mostly elbow length, with a frill, but this was now more often of plain muslin to match the fichu, instead of lace. Occasionally long sleeves were worn and they had a small frill at the wrist. In both cases the basic sleeves are used.

The skirt was no longer open at the front and the fullness was now at the back, giving a slight 'bustle' effect. The front was flatter so the two front pleats should be stitched down from underneath, and the skirt shortened here to show the shoes, but it remained long at the back. A small version of the padding used in Variation No. 7 will be needed to hold the back fullness out a little. Always adjust hems when padding is used as it inevitably lifts the skirt up a bit.

Aprons, embroidered or of flowered material were long, nearly reaching to the hem of the dress. They were worn by ladies of fashion, though the dainty elegance of these showed that they were worn for show, and not for work.

Hair was powdered until the late 1780's after which powder declined in favour, and the hair was worn brushed back from the forehead and held at the nape of the neck with a bow, the ends falling over the shoulders in one or two graceful ringlets. Paint, powder and patches were at the height of fashion during the seventies, after which they declined in favour till by 1790 they were rarely seen.

Jewellery. Diamonds and pearls were much used for hair ornaments and bracelets until the simpler styles set in, and bands of velvet or ruched ribbon continued to be worn round the throat till nearly the end of the century.

Suitable colours. In the early part of the reign yellows, light greens and blues were used, with additions of white material scattered with flowers in delicate shades. Later russet colours, brown and darker greens were worn as well, but now narrow stripes were fashionable as well as floral patterns.

Shoes were still pointed till about 1790, when a rounder toe began to be fashionable.

PLAYS

All of Sheridan's immediately spring to mind.
The Rivals and *The Duenna*, both in 1775
The School for Scandal, 1777
A Trip to Scarborough (taken from Vanbugh's *The Relapse*), 1777
The Critic, 1779
After which he entered Parliament and did not write again.
The Blue Cockade, 1780
Jackal, 1773–93
Berkeley Square, half modern, half eighteenth century

Variation No. 11. Regency, 1811. George IV, 1820–30

The basic bodice can still be used, especially in yellows, light blues, greens and greys, with blackberry and purple for older women, but one or two completely new dresses may have to be made in white if the play includes very young girls, and ball or evening wear is required.

When the basic bodice is used, enough of the same material will need to have been bought to make the quite different skirt, shown in Layout 3, f.p. 32). The skirt is sewn to the bodice just below the bust line, and must be pinned in place

REGENCY 1811. GEORGE IV. 1820-30.

MAKING-UP DIAGRAM No 26.

ATTACHING SKIRT TO BASIC BODICE.

BIND THE TOP OF THE SKIRT BEFORE SEWING UP DARTS OR SEAMS. THIS MAKES IT EASY TO ALTER SIZE OR FIT.

CENTRE FRONT

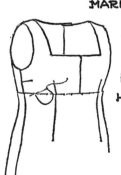

MARK WITH TACKING THREAD THE LINE TO WHICH THE SKIRT SHOULD BE SEWN. SEW IN PLACE BY HAND WITH A LONG HEMMING STITCH, USING DOUBLE THREAD.

on the figure as the size of the bust will alter the line. Using double thread, sew in place by hand with a short upper and long under hemming stitch (see Diagram 26, p. 77).

If an entirely new dress has to be made, use the basic bodice layout, but cut it a little shorter leaving enough turning at the bottom to allow for adjustments to bust size, make up as before described. The skirt is used either trimmed in various ways, or as an under-skirt when veiled with the very thin materials then fashionable.

Illustration 8, p. 79, shows several versions, in the earliest (1810) the basic dress is covered with 'muslin' and has a very Grecian look. For the 'muslin' use nylon curtain net, Voile or gauze in one of the man-made fabrics. Later the demand for warmer more practical clothes made the other changes come into fashion. For the long sleeve of the 1825 dress and the short jacket of 1815, use the long basic sleeve with a matching puffed sleeve gathered and sewn on at its lower edge, then turned back over itself and again gathered to the top of the basic sleeve. The same applies to the jacket sleeve, only the puffed section is longer, and gathered at a third place (see Layout 13 and Diagram 27, pp. 80–81, for jacket).

Many variations can be achieved by the use of different trimmings, ruching, and frills, so that no two dresses need look alike. The big, full sleeves of the 1820 dress should be made of thin, fairly stiff material, and the bodice trimmed with the gold and pearl braid which was so fashionable. This can be made of gold painted plain braid or lace insertion, and sewn with pearls. Here is one of the many uses for the junk jewellery so often to be found at Jumble Sales. A version of the dress for a young girl would have very short puffed sleeves and be in white, pale blue or pink. Both styles are for evening wear. Fill in some of the square neck if the dress is being used for day-time wear, with an edging which matches the trimming used on the skirt and/or at the high waist line. For the collared fill-in a modern blouse might easily be found, and a frill added to the collar; or if the collar is not suitable, use the layout for the smaller Puritan version in Variation No. 5, p. 54.

The *bonnet-hat* worn by the 1815 figure is made in the same way as the one fashionable in 1750–60, only make the crown one inch deeper, and trim with feathers instead of flowers. Another type of bonnet was beginning to be worn as shown on the 1825 figure (see Layout 13, p. 80), the brim became larger as time went on. It can be made in anything from cardboard to straw, the back part must be made of straw, which is more durable. If an old straw hat is used for the poke brim *always* sew binding or ribbon onto the marking line before cutting away the surplus straw, and for these bonnets a piece of hat wire should be button-holed to the edge in long stitches, before facing back the binding or ribbon (see Diagram 28, p. 85). The turban is very easy to make from an old gauze scarf: gather at the centre to about 4 inches wide, then twist the remainder of the scarf round the head tucking the ends neatly into place and securing with fine hairpins. Add some feathers made up into an elegant group, and fix these in place with either hairpins sewn to the feathers or with short hat pins. This style is only suitable for married or rather older women, young girls wore flowers and ribbons.

The *muff* is a straight piece of material about 15 inches wide and 30 inches long, join up the short width, interface with cotton wool, and line with inexpensive rayon taffeta. Finish with a trimming of fur or ruching at the edge of the muff, velvet would be suitable for both the muff and the ruching.

Hair was often cut short at the front to curl round the face, the back hair being caught up into curls on the top of the head, from where it fell in short ringlets. If additional hair is needed crêpe hair and the real hair will not mix unless it is a case of a small ringlet showing from beneath a hat or cap. Ribbon was frequently used to tie the hair at the top of the head, and the ends allowed to fall with the ringlets.

ILLUSTRATION No8.

REGENCY & GEORGE 1V.

1815.

1820.

1825.

1812.

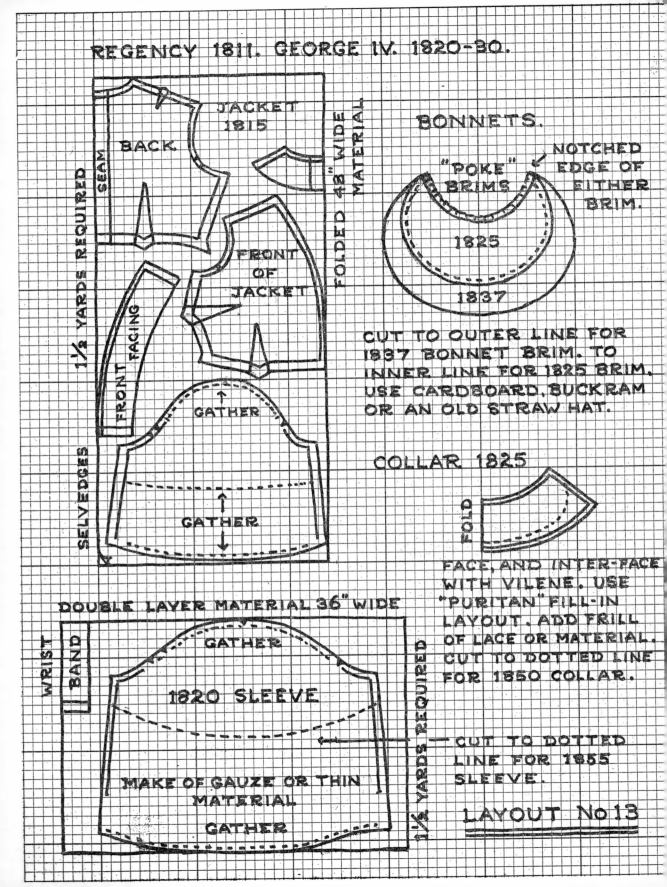

REGENCY 1811. GEORGE IV. 1820-30.

JACKET 1815

BACK

SEAM

1½ YARDS REQUIRED

FOLDED 48" WIDE MATERIAL

FRONT OF JACKET

FRONT FACING

SELVEDGES

GATHER

GATHER

BONNETS.

"POKE" BRIMS

NOTCHED EDGE OF EITHER BRIM.

1825

1837

CUT TO OUTER LINE FOR 1837 BONNET BRIM. TO INNER LINE FOR 1825 BRIM. USE CARDBOARD, BUCKRAM OR AN OLD STRAW HAT.

COLLAR 1825

FOLD

FACE, AND INTER-FACE WITH VILENE. USE "PURITAN" FILL-IN LAYOUT. ADD FRILL OF LACE OR MATERIAL. CUT TO DOTTED LINE FOR 1850 COLLAR.

DOUBLE LAYER MATERIAL 36" WIDE

WRIST BAND

GATHER

1820 SLEEVE

MAKE OF GAUZE OR THIN MATERIAL

GATHER

1½ YARDS REQUIRED

CUT TO DOTTED LINE FOR 1855 SLEEVE.

LAYOUT No 13

REGENCY 1811. GEORGE IV. 1820-30.

MAKING-UP DIAGRAM No 27.

(A)

SEW UP SEAMS
LEAVING SIDE AND
BACK SEAMS
"FREE" FOR
EASY SIZE
ADJUSTMENT.

BIND BOTTOM EDGE IN
SEPARATE SECTIONS.

JACKET 1815.

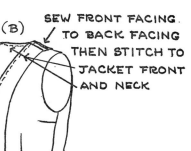

(B)

SEW FRONT FACING.
TO BACK FACING
THEN STITCH TO
JACKET FRONT
AND NECK

STITCH DARTS IN PLACE.

(C)

SEW BACK
FACING, USE
HERRING-
BONE
STITCH.
TURN UP
HEM AND
SEW INTO
PLACE. TRIM OUT·SIDE
WITH BRAID ON FACING LINE

INSIDE

SLEEVE OF JACKET.

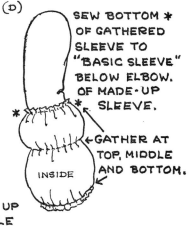

(D)

SEW BOTTOM ✱
OF GATHERED
SLEEVE TO
"BASIC SLEEVE"
BELOW ELBOW.
OF MADE-UP
SLEEVE.

←GATHER AT
TOP, MIDDLE
AND BOTTOM.

INSIDE

(E)

TURN GATHERED
SLEEVE UPWARDS.
ADJUST GATHERS
TO FIT ARM-HOLE,
SEW IN PLACE.
THE SAME METHOD
IS USED FOR THE
1825 SLEEVE.

DRAW UP
MIDDLE
GATHERS AND CATCH·
STITCH IN PLACE.

Jewellery was sometimes simple and in good taste, at other times it was ostentatious, so use it according to the character of the part. Bracelets were much worn as arms were barer than before.

Suitable colours. These have been described at the beginning of this Variation. Long stoles in gauze and thin silks were very much worn in the evenings by all ages.

Shoes were now flat, round toed and held on by crossed ribbons which tied round the ankles.

PLAYS

This is a period rich in plays for 'Women Only' many based on the works of Jane Austen, there are also 3 act mixed cast plays made from her books.

Quality Street, 1810
Penny for a Song, 1810
I have Five Daughters, 1813 ⎫ both based on Jane Austen's books
Pride and Prejudice, 1813 ⎭
Man with a Load of Mischief, 1815 (approx.)
The Anatomist, 1828
Granite
Mr. Crummies' Presents, 1830

Variation No. 12.   Victorian, 1837–50 (first period)

Even before Victoria came to the throne the fitted bodice and full skirt were back on the fashion scene, the high waist came gradually down to the natural waist line, and skirts grew fuller, but at first only prettily so. Muslins and very thin cottons, so fashionable during the Regency, gave way to thicker fabrics, such as fine woollens, silks, and velvets, and cashmere shawls began their long popularity. As a young Queen, Victoria was gay and loved dancing; it was only after she married that she became so sedate and serious. This, and the rise of a solid respectable middle-class, set the tone of the fashions: even the drawings in 'La Mode' simpered. Later in the seventies dramatists such as Hendrik Ibsen (1828–1906) began to crack open the moral façade of the times, followed by George Bernard Shaw in the nineties, when his plays were first produced, though he had written some much earlier.

In this first period the fashions were very attractive, the bodice was a V from a widened shoulder to a small, neat waist, the effect being achieved by a shawl-like collar that ended at the centre front waistline (see Illustration 9, p. 83, 1837, dress). The required addition could be made of material to match the basic dress and trimmed with a darker shade, but many variations of colouring will suggest themselves, and will give the needed change to suit the characters in the play (see Layout 14, p. 86 and Diagram 29, p. 87 for additions). The shawl-collar is sewn in place as before described, double thread and a hemming stitch, but leave the outer edge over the sleeve free, only stitching the front part of this edge at the bust line. A *vestee* of fine cambric with a rolled collar was often worn inside the neck-line if the dress is for day-time wear (see Diagram 29).

VICTORIAN.

1837.

1875.

1870.

1860.

1855.

1850.

1885.

ILLUSTRATION No. 9.

The sleeve was tight from the wrist to just below the elbow, where it billowed out into a full top section. The sleeve should be of the same material as the dress, for this the basic sleeve can be used, lapped over from the wrist and hooked in place to fit the arm. Then a matching full section is gathered on below the elbow, and gathered again to fit the arm-hole. Use Layout 13, p. 80, for the puffed sleeve section of the 1815 jacket, only omit the middle row of gathers. Short puffed sleeves were worn for the evening.

The *Poke bonnet* continued in fashion and was lavishly trimmed with curled ostrich feathers, ribbons and flowers, and tied under the chin with matching ribbons. It is made in the same way as the 1825 bonnet, but with a wider, deeper 'poke', the crown of an old straw hat can be combined with a cardboard poke brim covered with rayon taffeta, stuck in place with copydex, and edged with a paper frill, if a large enough straw brim is not available. The ribbons, flowers and feathers will conceal the join, as well as nearly all the crown (see Layout 14, p. 86, and Diagram 28, p. 85, for 1825, using larger brim layout).

Hair was arranged in curls round the face, and the rest combed back into a bun at the crown of the head. Feathers or flowers were worn in the evening pinned to the bun.

Jewellery. Very little was used; ear-rings went out because the curls covered the ears, bracelets were worn in the evening.

Suitable colours. Pale shades were fashionable, so the yellows, blues and lighter greens and of course greys will be used. To get the pale effect keep the additions to soft tones, a few darker dresses for older people; age made a great difference in dress, it is only now-a-days that mothers and daughters can 'swop' dresses.

Shoes either flat with roundish toe, or with small heel, very like a modern bedroom slipper, some had a narrow edge of ruched ribbon with a bow at the front. The top was a court shoe line.

PLAYS

Any play about the early years of Victoria's reign, her Coronation, and meeting with Albert.

Portrait of a Queen (for the early scenes of this play)

Variation No. 13.   Victorian, 1850–65 (second period)

As the reign progressed the skirts became wider and wider, till by 1860 a fashionable woman looked like a walking pyramid that ended in a flounce, or contrasting material and rows of braid. To hold out the wider skirt the crinoline was invented, but even if one can be made or the real thing borrowed, they are as hard to manage on the stage as a real farthingale. Both have a disconcerting way of seesawing, especially when the actress sits down, and without a lot of practice disaster can easily happen. Funny for the audience but not for the actress! The separate petticoat described in Variation No. 8, p. 63, will need an increasing number of frills (these can still be of crêpe paper) but by 1860 the skirt was so wide at the bottom that a deep, stiff edge must be added. For this a double fold of millinery nylon net, having a finished width of 8 or 9 inches, should be sewn

BONNETS 1825, 1837 AND 1850.

MAKING-UP DIAGRAM No 28.

(A)

UNDER SIDE

NOTCH EDGE

(B)

1825.

CUT COVERING MATERIAL ¾" LARGER THAN BRIM. TURN OVER ONTO UNDER SIDE, AND STICK IN PLACE. COVER UNDER SIDE WITH SLIGHTLY GATHERED CREPE PAPER OR MATERIAL. SEW IN PLACE WITH A LONG BACK-STITCH.

* BIND EDGE OF STRAW CROWN. SEW IN PLACE BY HAND. COVER NOTCHES ON INSIDE WITH RIBBON.

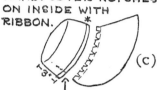

(C)

LEAVE 3" GAP AT CENTRE BACK WHEN SEWING BRIM TO CROWN. MAKE 1837 BONNET BY THE SAME METHOD.

1837.

COVER UNDER SIDE OF BRIM WITH PLAIN MATERIAL AND RUCHING AT EDGE, OR GATHER -ED AS FOR 1825 BONNET.

COVER NOTCHED EDGE WITH RIBBON.

1850.

CUT COVERING MATERIAL ¾" LARGER ALL ROUND. TURN OVER NOTCHED EDGES AND STICK IN PLACE.

(A)

(B)

BACK

COVER TWO LAYERS NYLON NET ON BOTH SIDES WITH MATERIAL.

SEW UP DART, FACE BOTTOM EDGE WITH BIAS MATERIAL.

(C)

SEW "POKE" TO BACK BY HAND.

COVER FRONT OF INNER SIDE. TURN IN NARROW HEM, SLIP-STITCH ALONG EDGE

(D)

STICK SELF ADHESIVE FABLON HERE, SEALING EDGE OF FRONT FACING AND NOTCHED BACK EDGE.

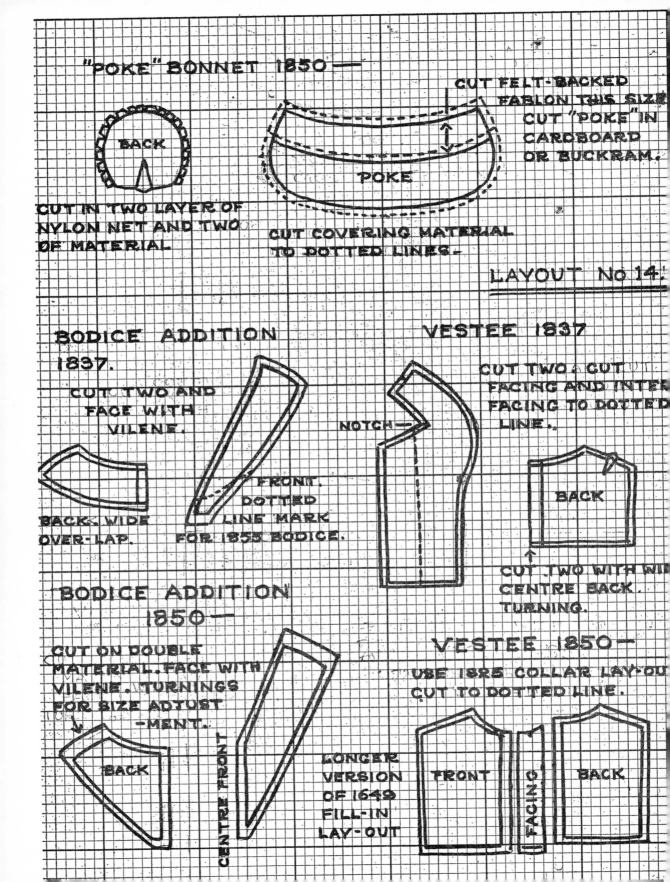

"POKE" BONNET 1850 —

BACK

CUT IN TWO LAYER OF
NYLON NET AND TWO
OF MATERIAL.

CUT FELT-BACKED
FABLON THIS SIZE.
CUT "POKE" IN
CARDBOARD
OR BUCKRAM.

POKE

CUT COVERING MATERIAL
TO DOTTED LINES.

LAYOUT No 14.

BODICE ADDITION 1837.

CUT TWO AND
FACE WITH
VILENE.

BACK WIDE
OVER-LAP.

FRONT.
DOTTED
LINE MARK
FOR 1855 BODICE.

VESTEE 1837

CUT TWO & CUT
FACING AND INTER
FACING TO DOTTED
LINE.

NOTCH→

BACK

CUT TWO WITH WID
CENTRE BACK
TURNING.

BODICE ADDITION 1850 —

CUT ON DOUBLE
MATERIAL. FACE WITH
VILENE. TURNINGS
FOR SIZE ADJUST
-MENT.

BACK

CENTRE FRONT

VESTEE 1850 —

USE 1825 COLLAR LAY-OU
CUT TO DOTTED LINE.

LONGER
VERSION
OF 1649
FILL-IN
LAY-OUT

FRONT

FACING

BACK

VICTORIAN. 1837— FIRST PERIOD.

"SHAWL" BODICE ADDITION. 1837.

(A)

SEW IN THE SLEEVE. USE 1815 LAY-OUT, BUT ONLY GATHER AT THE TOP AND BOTTOM.

SMALL DART

HEM THE EDGES OF FRONT AND BACK SECTIONS. THEN JOIN AT SHOULDER SEAM. OVER-SEW.

CUT TWO STRIPS OF MATERIAL ON BIAS, 5" WIDE, ABOUT 30" LONG. DART ON SHOULDER, AND SEW TO "SHAWL" ADDITION. COLOUR SHOULD BLEND WITH DRESS.

VESTEE 1837.

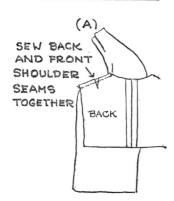

(A)

SEW BACK AND FRONT SHOULDER SEAMS TOGETHER

BACK

MAKING-UP DIAGRAM No 29.

(B)

JOIN COLLAR AT CENTRE BACK. CUT NOTCH (SEE LAY-OUT) AND SEW COLLAR TO BACK, NOTCH TURNING. HEM EDGES.

SEW FACING AND INTER-FACING TO UNDER-SIDE OF COLLAR. TURN RIGHT-SIDE OUT AND PRESS. SEW BUTTONS OVER SNAP FASTENERS ON THE FRONT.

(C)

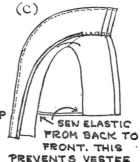

SEW ELASTIC FROM BACK TO FRONT. THIS PREVENTS VESTEE FROM RIDING UP.

on top of the skirt, making quite sure that it is not nearer than ½ inch to the skirt edge. This is so that it won't catch on stockings and tear them. The net must then be masked with a frill or pleated edging (see Illustration 9, p. 83, 1860 dress).

To return to the 1850's when the skirt was still only attractively full, the fitted bodice continued to have the deep pointed V line from shoulder to the small waist, but it was now less like a shawl collar, and more a section in contrasting material, the same was used to trim the skirt. The V neck thus formed was filled in with embroidered linen, for which ornamental nylon curtain net will be a good substitute. This would be suitable for evening wear, for the day a vestee type fill-in with a small collar would have been worn, and for this a check or tartan material would be a good choice, as they were very fashionable, the same material should be used for the under sleeve. They reflect the interest and love which Queen Victoria and Prince Albert had for Scotland; indeed they may be said to have started the tartan craze which is still one of Scotland's biggest exports. A typical sleeve of this period was set smoothly into the armhole and belled out just below the elbow, ending in an indented curve on the upper part of the arm, with an edging of the same material as was used for the V bodice addition. The under sleeve, which should be made as a separate article, is the same width as the main sleeve, and should be sewn in place by hand, then gathered in to fit the wrist and finished with a narrow band (see Layout 15, p. 90 and Diagrams 30 and 31, pp. 91 and 93, for V bodice addition and bell sleeve).

The Poke bonnet was now much smaller and narrower, rather the shape of a flower pot with a third of it sliced away. It can be made of cardboard covered with material, but must then be lined in the head part with some non slippery fabric, such as felt backed Fablon to prevent it slipping on the head. These bonnets were more simply trimmed, a ribbon usually went over the top and tied under the chin, a bow or small bunch of flowers might be added (see Layout 14, p. 86 and Diagram 28, p. 85 for making).

Hair was smooth and parted in the middle, curving over the ears and coiled into a bun at the back of the head.

Victoria's was a very long reign and fashion had begun to change more quickly. The very wide skirt of 1860 has already been described, but the style of the bodice changed also. A plastron-like addition is made of two cut off V shaped pieces of material, joined at the shoulder and fitting up to the neck. The back V must be in two sections and fit onto the basic dress down the back opening (see Layout 15, p. 90, and Diagram 31, p. 93). The faced edge of the *plastron* is turned over and hemmed by hand, adjusting for size; a trimming of matching braid may be added, then it is slip-stitched all round onto the basic dress, leaving a few inches at the shoulder unsewn until the sleeve is set in. A narrow band or pleated frill is added to the high neck-line. Use either the same material as the basic dress, or for richer people taffeta or a stiff cotton velveteen in a matching colour or slightly darker shade. Whatever kind of pleated flounce, frill, or other trimming is used at the bottom of the skirt it should be repeated on a smaller scale at the end of the bell sleeve.

Headwear had changed drastically; the *pork-pie hat* was all the rage, these are easy to make from the crown of a straw or felt hat. If straw, mould as described for the 1750 hat (p. 74); if felt, steam over boiling water, then mould in the same way. Trim with a long curled feather, looped-up ribbons or swathed material. (See Illustration 9, p. 83, 1860 lady, holding hat, also Diagram 31, p. 93).

Hair. This had also changed in style though it was still smooth and parted in the middle, it was now held at the back in a coarse net. This was sometimes made of chenille.

Jewellery. Large oval or round brooches were worn at the high necks, and longish ear-rings were fashionable in the 1860's, and also for evening wear in the earlier period.

Suitable colours. All the basic colours are right but pale shades should be used to make additions for evening wear in the early part of the period. Later brighter greens and blues would be more suitable, and, as has been said, tartans and checks in bright mixtures were very much worn, especially during the day. Darker colours were more favoured later, but russets and greens are still right and if addition either match or are a slightly darker tone this gives the rather more sober effect required.

Shoes remained flat or with very small heels, short boots were in, but as the skirts literally swept the floors these need not be made, as the feet were so rarely seen.

PLAYS

There are so many only a very few can be mentioned.
The Barretts of Wimpole Street
A Christmas Carol
Jane Eyre, 1850
Lady with a Lamp, 1848 to 1860 section
Little Women, 1860–5
Portrait of a Queen, 1850–65 section
Trelawney of the Wells, 1860
Wild Decembers, 1845–55

Variation No. 14. Victorian, 1870–85 (third period)

This period saw the return of the bustle, though at first the skirt was just padded out a little as with the 1790 dress. Later the bodice was lengthened in the front and a deep drape attached that went across the front of the dress, and was caught up at the back to give a marked 'bustle' effect. Use the same padding as was described in Variation No. 7, p. 62 for both these styles. With the early style very decorative aprons were worn.

To make the draped *bustle* addition, you will also need a plastron for which the 1860 Layout 15, p. 90, can be used; the same material should be used for this and the bustle drape. Cut a curved section according to the layout, this must be lined (an old piece of sheet will do) and be larger than the top section to the extent of 12 inches at the centre front curving to the same size over the side-back. Onto the top curved section sew a piece of the material with a finished width of 26 inches, and a minimum length of 92 inches, making 2 or 3 small tucks over the hips to make it drape well. Gather into deep pleats at the back, and hook together with two large hooks and eyes. The rest of the drape will then fall in

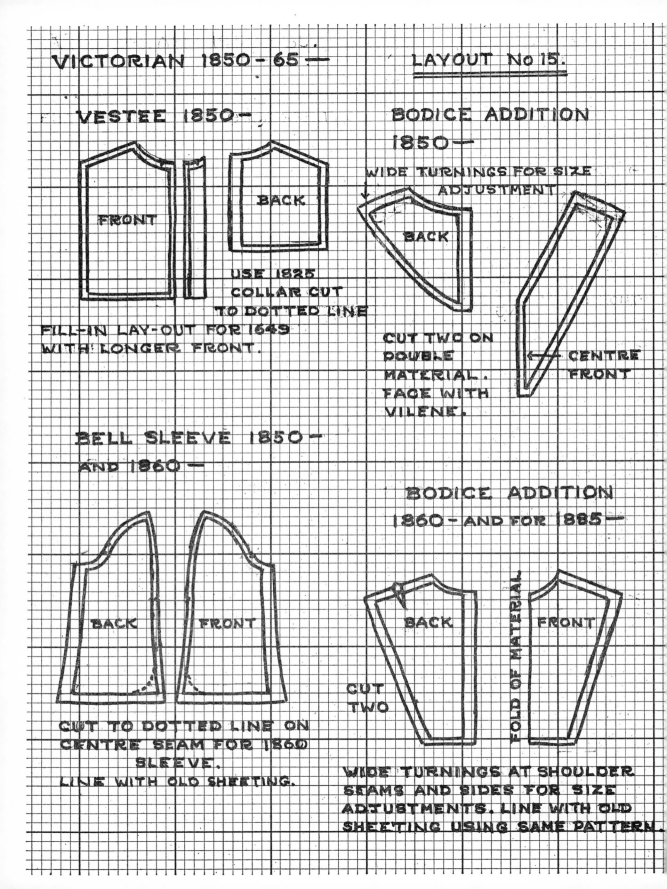

VICTORIAN 1850-65 —

VESTEE 1850 —

FRONT

BACK

USE 1825 COLLAR CUT TO DOTTED LINE

FILL-IN LAY-OUT FOR 1649 WITH LONGER FRONT.

BODICE ADDITION 1850 —

WIDE TURNINGS FOR SIZE ADJUSTMENT

BACK

← CENTRE FRONT

CUT TWO ON DOUBLE MATERIAL. FACE WITH VILENE.

BELL SLEEVE 1850 — AND 1860 —

BACK   FRONT

CUT TO DOTTED LINE ON CENTRE SEAM FOR 1860 SLEEVE. LINE WITH OLD SHEETING.

BODICE ADDITION 1860 — AND FOR 1885 —

BACK   FRONT

CUT TWO

FOLD OF MATERIAL

WIDE TURNINGS AT SHOULDER SEAMS AND SIDES FOR SIZE ADJUSTMENTS. LINE WITH OLD SHEETING USING SAME PATTERN.

VICTORIAN. 1850-65. SECOND PERIOD.

MAKING-UP DIAGRAM No 30.

BODICE ADDITION.

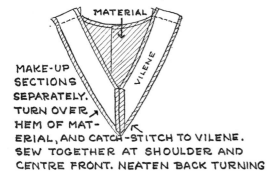

MAKE-UP SECTIONS SEPARATELY. TURN OVER HEM OF MATERIAL, AND CATCH-STITCH TO VILENE. SEW TOGETHER AT SHOULDER AND CENTRE FRONT. NEATEN BACK TURNING

TRIM WITH LACE OR EMBRIODERY FOR MORE "DRESSY" WEAR.

BELL SLEEVE 1850 AND 1860.

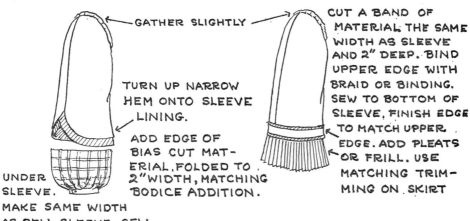

GATHER SLIGHTLY

TURN UP NARROW HEM ONTO SLEEVE LINING.

ADD EDGE OF BIAS CUT MATERIAL, FOLDED TO 2" WIDTH, MATCHING BODICE ADDITION.

UNDER SLEEVE. MAKE SAME WIDTH AS BELL SLEEVE. SEW INTO PLACE ON SLEEVE LINING.

CUT A BAND OF MATERIAL THE SAME WIDTH AS SLEEVE AND 2" DEEP. BIND UPPER EDGE WITH BRAID OR BINDING. SEW TO BOTTOM OF SLEEVE, FINISH EDGE TO MATCH UPPER EDGE. ADD PLEATS OR FRILL. USE MATCHING TRIMMING ON SKIRT

a graceful cascade over the back of the skirt. Next pin the folds of the drape in place onto the lining extention, where it should be sewn with a few long back-stitches, the long stitch being underneath, of course. This arrangement acts as a 'stay' and prevents the folds from falling over the knees when the actress sits down, for if this does happen it may well prevent her from getting up! (see Layout 16, p. 94, and Diagrams 32A-D, p. 95). Curtains, either flowered or plain are useful for this addition as it does require a good deal of material. If new stuff has to be bought, stiff fairly cheap rayon will do as this is not for a basic dress, only an addition. Look on market stalls; if you explain your needs people are often very helpful.

Clothes were often lavishly trimmed at this time with braid, fringe and ruching, sometimes with more enthusiasm than taste. Fringe should be looked for at Jumble Sales on old curtains, then dyed to requirements, and straight binding is always a good substitute for braid. Use magenta and bright violet when possible for these trimmings, as they were both colours typical of the period.

The sleeves were long and straight, often with a cuff trimmed to match the dress, and edged with a frill of cambric or lace, which should be repeated at the high neck-band. Dresses of contrasting colours were a feature of this period, but on the stage care must be taken that the contrast is not too violent if an actress is small, or broad and rather plump. Two tones of the same colour, a flowered material, or a tartan that blends with the colour of the basic dress would be best in such cases. Be careful about using very shiny fabrics as they catch the strong lights, and show up unfortunate curves in a very unbecoming way. Incidentally this also applies to modern clothes.

Hats were small and in a great variety of styles and so adorned with feathers and flowers that their shape is hardly seen. Some were tied under the chin with a bow of ribbon. A shallow version of the pork-pie hat was curved from front to back instead of straight, another and later style had a small upturned brim, this hat was perched on top of the head and held on with ribbons. Many hats found at Jumble Sales are easily adapted to these fashions.

Hair was swept up from the sides of the face to the crown of the head and held there, often with a flat bow of ribbon. From this point plaits or ringlets fell to the nape of the neck; the plaits would have been looped up, and ringlets are only suitable for young women and girls.

Jewellery. Rings and brooches were amongst the most popular articles of adornment though ear-rings were still worn. Garnets, rubies and pearls were much favoured. All settings should be gold; it was imitated if the real thing could not be afforded. Platinum had not come into use till years later.

Suitable colours. All the basic colours are still worn, but in the early part of this period ally them with soft shades, but later use harsher shades of green, violet and magenta.

Shoes were still little seen and had not changed to any great degree.

PLAYS

A period rich in plays, some written then and some having been written about those times.

The Lady with a Lamp, 1870–85 section
Portrait of a Queen, 1870–85 section
Pink String and Sealing Wax, 1880

VICTORIAN. 1850 – 65.

MAKING-UP DIAGRAM. No 31.

BODICE ADDITION 1860 –

(B)

(A)

SEW LINING TO MATERIAL AT SIDES, BOTTOM AND DOWN CENTRE BACK OPENING. TURN RIGHT-SIDE OUT AND PRESS. THEN SEW UP SHOULDER SEAMS. ADJUST TO FIT FIGURE IF NECESSARY.

TURN OVER HEM AT SIDES AND BOTTOM, SEW IN PLACE.

NECK TRIMMING.

(C)

BIND EDGE OF NECK WITH NARROW BAND, CUT ON STRAIGHT OF MATERIAL. ADD STIFFENED PLEATING OR LACE. A BOW AND BUTTON CAN BE ADDED.

PORK-PIE HATS

CUT OFF CROWN, BIND EDGE WITH MATCH-ING BINDING. FLATTEN TOP IF NECESSARY. (METHOD AS FOR 1750 HAT.) IF CROWN IS FELT, STEAM OVER BOILING WATER, THEN SHAPE. ALTERNATIVE TRIMMING.

The Dolls House, 1875
Ghosts, 1881
An Enemy of the People, 1882   } all by Hendrik Ibsen
The Wild Duck, 1884, etc.
Gaslight, 1885
The Right Honourable Gentleman, 1885
Many plays by Pinero and Tchehov come into the latter part of this period so this can only be a short list.

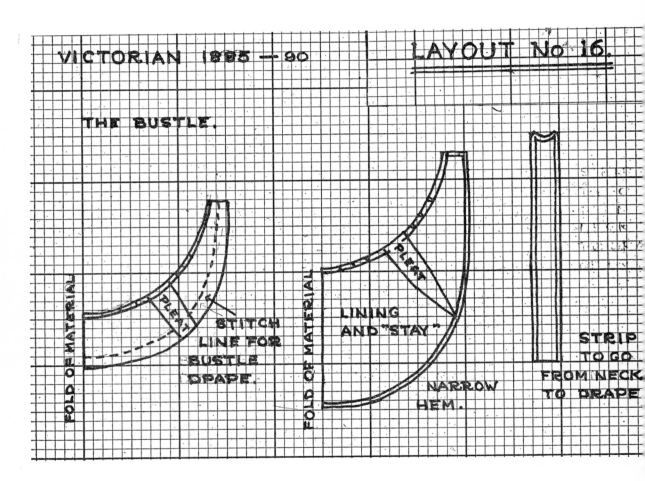

VICTORIAN. 1870-85.

MAKE-UP DIAGRAM No 32.   ## THE BUSTLE.

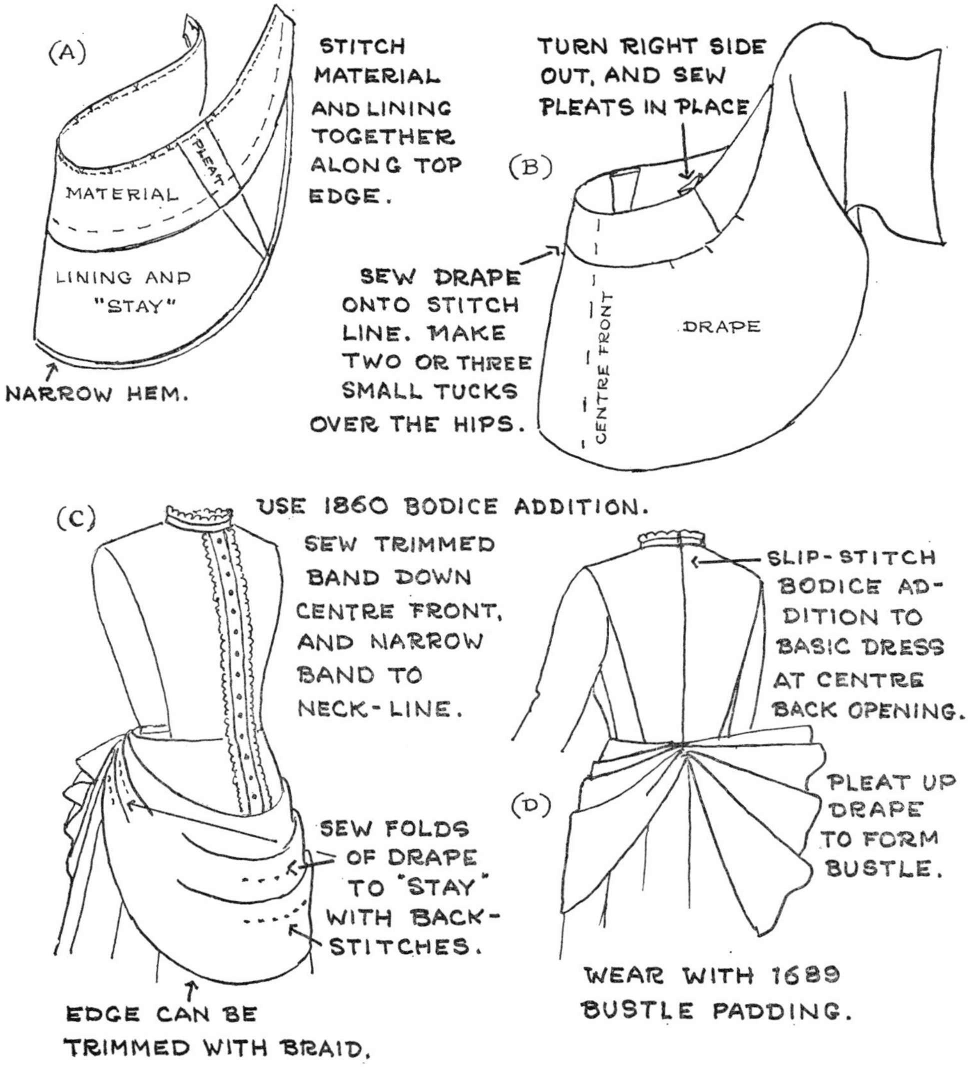

(A)

STITCH
MATERIAL
AND LINING
TOGETHER
ALONG TOP
EDGE.

PLEAT

MATERIAL

LINING AND
"STAY"

NARROW HEM.

SEW DRAPE
ONTO STITCH
LINE. MAKE
TWO OR THREE
SMALL TUCKS
OVER THE HIPS.

TURN RIGHT SIDE
OUT, AND SEW
PLEATS IN PLACE

(B)

CENTRE FRONT

DRAPE

(C)

USE 1860 BODICE ADDITION.

SEW TRIMMED
BAND DOWN
CENTRE FRONT,
AND NARROW
BAND TO
NECK-LINE.

SEW FOLDS
OF DRAPE
TO "STAY"
WITH BACK-
STITCHES.

EDGE CAN BE
TRIMMED WITH BRAID.

SLIP-STITCH
BODICE AD-
DITION TO
BASIC DRESS
AT CENTRE
BACK OPENING.

(D)

PLEAT UP
DRAPE
TO FORM
BUSTLE.

WEAR WITH 1889
BUSTLE PADDING.